CANINE ENRI

The book your dog needs you to read

Canine Enrichment
THE BOOK YOUR DOG NEEDS YOU TO READ
Shay Kelly BSc FdSc

Graphic design and cover photo: Shay Kelly

ISBN: 9781088600191

If you find typographical errors in this book, they were purposely placed as enrichment for those who enjoy finding them.

For all who read this book and make the world a better place for dogs.

Notes from the Author:

I'm occasionally sent products to test, review or advise on; but I'm not a salesperson. Products mentioned in this book are done so with the upmost integrity. I do not receive any payment for advising on or recommending any product.

Throughout this book I refer to dogs as 'him'. This is purely for ease of writing and is not intended to infer preference of any sort.

To those who gave help, advice, support or encouragement during the writing of this book, I thank you:

Alex Clark

Caroline Kelly

Denise O'Moore

Diane Kasperowicz

Ellis Kelly

Kate Mallatratt

Kim Kaye

Linda Case

Marta Young

Matt Kelly

Sarah Fisher

Steve Mann

Sue Ketland

Susan Friedman

Tony Cruse

Thank you to all the members of my Canine Enrichment Facebook group. You are the people who have changed the world for dogs. You are the people who have made enrichment commonplace.

Thank you to the admins (past and present) of the enrichment group. I am eternally grateful for all that you do.

And finally, thank you to the staff of Bishop Burton College for setting me free.

Contents

Introduction

When we bring a dog into our lives we buy a lead, a bowl, a bed, and a few brightly coloured toys. We might think about training. We definitely think about toilet training. We don't tend to think much past this. Why do we want a dog in our lives? Because we think it will be fun? Companionship? To go walking and stay healthy? Just because we do? For most of us, it just feels right and for sure, the way dogs seem to unashamedly adore us is a real thrill.

We get dogs because we think they will improve our lives. But what about their lives? Do we stop to consider what the dog needs? We often don't. The most common cause given for dogs under two years of age to be put to sleep is behaviour problems. In most cases, these dogs were not born significantly different from any other dogs of their type. They were simply let down by humans who couldn't, wouldn't, or just didn't consider meeting their needs.

In 2017 I founded a Facebook group, named Canine Enrichment, to raise awareness of the need to provide a meaningful life for our companion dogs. I didn't expect it to get much interest. In the early days it even attracted a fair few critics. One particular comment is etched in my mind.

A meaningful life? They're just dogs!

I needed no more motivation to change this mindset and make enrichment common place; not an afterthought, but something everybody automatically considers. In the following two years the group membership grew beyond belief to 200,000 members. It was being recommended by vets, behaviourists, dog walkers, trainers, and rehoming centre staff. My faith in humans wanting to do the best by their companion animals was somewhat restored. I was of course bombarded with every question going; more than I could ever hope to answer. So here it is, the what, why, where and when of canine enrichment, according to Shay Kelly.

What is Canine Enrichment?

Enrichment is the action of improving the quality of something. But what are we improving the quality of? We're improving the quality of life; our dog's life. What an amazingly privileged position we find ourselves in. We get to decide what sort of life our canine companion gets. There may be all sorts of things we can't control, for example, ill health. But whatever ailments, disabilities, or predispositions a dog may or may not have, we still get to influence things. We still get to enrich their lives. We still get to do the best we can for them.

Improving the quality of their lives, still doesn't really tell us much though does it? According to this definition, almost anything could be called enrichment. Are vaccinations enrichment? How about nail trimming? Maybe a tooth extraction? These things certainly improve the dog's life, but they are not things the dog would usually choose to engage in. Some talented people have managed to make nail clipping a pleasant experience which the dog is only too willing to engage in, but for most dogs, they'd prefer not to bother. But canine enrichment isn't about things which merely keep the dog alive or pain-free; important as these things are. Canine enrichment is providing activities your dog eagerly wants to participate in. But hang on a moment; dogs may want to participate in many activities which aren't beneficial to long term health. We can't just allow dogs to do whatever they please and call it enrichment. Many dogs would love to remain off-lead, or eat too much food, or chase the neighbour's cat across the road. We are obviously not going to pronounce these things to be enrichment. They endanger life, not enrich it. So what are we left with? Canine enrichment is the act of providing low-risk activities in which the dog actively wants to participate. It's giving dogs something interesting to do. It's lighting a spark. It's giving them an engaging and fulfilling life.

More than ethics: You are already reading this book so I'm guessing you're already sold on the idea that providing your dog with an interesting life might be a good and ethical thing to do. But there are greater benefits than simply knowing we're doing the right thing by our dogs. A huge contributing factor of behaviour problems in dogs is the lack of appropriate stimulation. If we don't employ the dog's fantastically advanced brain, it may become self-employed and seek out any opportunity for stimulation.

In addition to giving dogs interesting things to do and keeping their minds actively engaged in appropriate behaviours, enrichment activities are particularly good for building the dog-human relationship. There's no pressure. There's no trying to get the dog to do something. There's no frustrated guardian. We're not looking for compliance. We're just offering an opportunity for the dog to have a good time. Each time we offer this opportunity we're adding to the amount of good experiences the dog associates with us. We need these positive experiences to massively outnumber the negative ones, such as going to the vets, nail trims, or when we accidentally step on a paw. We want at least one-hundred positive associations for every negative association. That sounds like a lot, but later in the book we'll see how easy it is to get these adding up.

The reason we want at least 100-1 is that negative experiences can be extremely powerful forces. Animals are hard wired to avoid danger. There are exceptions. For example, it doesn't come without risk for lions to hunt. But that is do or die. Another exception is the extremely powerful urge to mate. Many animals will fight and risk life threatening injuries for a mating partner. But again, this is about survival. Survival not of the individual, but of the genetic coding within the individual. And if that wasn't such a high priority, I wouldn't be here writing this book and you wouldn't be there reading it. The same innate urge to survive is what forces our dogs to avoid danger. If something frightens the dog, it's because (in the dog's mind) it could be dangerous. If something hurts the dog, it could be dangerous. If something's a little uncomfortable, or restrictive or novel, guess what? It could be dangerous. Fear of any dangerous situation is infinitely more powerful than a mere pleasant experience or something interesting to do because it's what keeps dogs alive, or at least it's what kept their ancestors alive long enough to pass on their genes. Something worth noting about genetic coding is that it's what made our ancestors successful in their environment. It's not necessarily beneficial to the environment we find ourselves in today. I'm not sure what function blushing ever served to my ancestors, but in the environment I grew up in, I could have done without it thank you very much! When the dog associates us with lots of pleasant experiences, we're building a trust fund. Sometimes bad things happen and that's life, but if we've saved enough in the trust fund, a small withdrawal won't feel so bad. Our trust fund (or relationship) will remain healthy.

Why Dogs Need Enrichment

Reason 1: Growing up in the 1970s in the small town of Stalybridge, eight miles to the east of Manchester, it was perfectly normal to see dogs wandering around the streets. These were not homeless dogs. These were dogs which had homes to go to but were allowed to roam at will. They'd walk around, meeting up with other dogs, sometimes forming large groups and then at some time or another they'd all go their separate ways and find their way back home. Not all dogs were roamers. I do remember the odd one or two which were kept indoors and only walked on a lead. But I think it's fair to say it was the norm and I know it was the norm in many other places too.

Back in the day, this way of living was much safer (but not without risk) than it would be today. There was far less traffic. In my street of approximately twenty-five properties it was quite rare to see a car. I don't remember ever seeing the dogs fight between themselves or bite anyone. The dogs were very well socialised and at ease with their environment. There was never a mention of the many behaviour problems we hear about today. But things have changed. For very good reasons dogs are now usually kept safely indoors. Another change is that we now have many families where all adult members need to go to work. Dogs may often be left for long periods with little to do and lacking social contact. Comparing how dogs used to live, to how they live today, I'm in no doubt that there's a behavioural void and that if this void is not filled with appropriate stimulation, behaviour problems will arise.

Reason 2: Google 'zoo enrichment' and it will soon become clear that enrichment for captive animals is a big deal. Gone are the days (at least in modern zoos) of keeping desperately depressed animals in barren enclosures. Zoos now go to extraordinary lengths to provide enrichment activities and environments which allow animals to practise their natural behaviour patterns and fulfil physiological and psychological needs. I make no argument here either in support or opposition of keeping animals in zoos. The stark reality is that, like it or not, we do keep millions of animals in zoos and whilst this practice continues, we have a moral duty to do the very best we can to meet their needs and give them the best life possible.

We absolutely expect and demand this of our zoos. Should it not also be the minimum expected for our dogs and other companion animals? It comes as a shock to many people when I suggest that our dogs are captive animals. But think about it for a moment; they don't choose who they get to live with. They don't have the option of changing their legal owner; they don't get to choose their environment, how many walks they get, their diet, their training class, etc. I don't mean to suggest that we are holding them against their will. They've evolved to live alongside humans and we could hardly abandon them now. But a dog's life is a lottery, it's total chance what life they are given and they're powerless to change it. However, it's a very special lottery because you get to choose whether your dog is a winner.

Reason 3: Mental stimulation is vitally important to brain development and good health. Some rather distasteful experiments during the 1960s demonstrated that suturing a cat's eye shut during the first three months of development rendered the cat permanently blind in that eye. The very idea of such an experiment, in my view, seems ridiculously cruel and unethical. But this was early evidence of how neural pathways are dependent on stimulation. Similar experiments have shown that cats which were only permitted to see horizontal lines didn't develop the ability to see vertical lines and vice versa.

The phenomenon of neuroplasticity is beyond doubt. It's how you, and I, and every animal on the planet is able to learn and adapt to our environments. It's how you are able to learn about the need to enrich your dog's life and it's how we can all influence dog behaviour with appropriate stimulation. Neuroplasticity is not only present during early development but throughout life. Such is the power of mental stimulation that it's commonly used to help stroke victims recover some lost abilities following damage to the brain. This is largely dependent on the severity and location of the damage, but that the brain can relearn some lost abilities is certain.

Enrichment activities are often used to comfort and enrich people with dementia. The Alzheimer's Society provides a 'singing for the brain' service which empowers people to express themselves. Seemingly, melody and song lyrics seem particularly resistant to dementia. I don't believe that dogs have much awareness of melody, but what's important is that we provide an outlet for brain activity. When I see an elderly dog sniffing, I can't help but think of it as a canine version of singing for the brain.

Reason 4: Humans quite like to be enriched. We have music, television, radio, computers, mobile phones, books, magazines, blogs, computer games, board games, mind games, employment, hobbies, shopping, fashion, cooking, eating out, sweets, chocolates, theatre, opera, chatting, singing, driving, gardening, companion animals, friends, Facebook, Twitter, photography, coffee, alcohol, poetry, holidays, jigsaw puzzles, hundreds of sports, languages, culture, art, education, you name it, we've got it.

What have dogs got? Only what we give them. Whilst it's obviously true that dogs do not need all the things that humans have, they still need a mentally stimulating environment in order to flourish. Our modern lives are full, often too full, but a dog's is often empty, far too empty. It may be that your dog is able to go to work with you, or that you're a very active person and the dog goes everywhere with you. You may be keen on heelwork to music, agility, or any one of the many canine sports or activities. It may be that your dog already has an interesting and active life. But for far more, life resembles laying around the house all day (often alone), going for a quick walk in the evening (if you're one of the lucky ones) and maybe having a couple of belly rubs as the human companion watches television. In fact, studies have indicated that up to 60 percent of companion dogs don't even get a regular walk. That's almost zero mental or physical activity. We can do better than this can't we? We must do better than this.

I don't write the above with a superiority complex, I'm as human as the next person. I work, I get tired, I get moody, I don't want to get wet, I have a headache, sore feet, and I completed two part time degree courses whilst working full time. My dogs' needs have not always been met as well as they could have been. But excuses don't improve a dog's life. Excuses don't give them anything to stimulate their amazing brains. This is why I've included a section on working enrichment into a busy life.

Reason 5: What is behaviour for? What's the point of it? The whole point of behaviour is to allow animals to seek appetitives (good stuff) and avoid aversives (bad stuff). I wish I could say that I came up with this simple explanation of the basic function of behaviour but I didn't. I heard it from Dr Susan Friedman at a behaviour seminar. Susan, of course, had put it far more eloquently.

What is behaviour for? It is to operate on the environment to get reinforcers and avoid aversive stimuli. Behaviour is for effect, that is, being effective at controlling outcomes.

I missed the next hour or so of what Susan said because I just sat there and pondered her words. The ridiculously complex science of behaviour had been stripped down to its basic function. Animals have an overwhelming need to perform behaviours. It's what they were built for. What would be the point of carrying around a heavy brain which consumes large amounts of energy, if they didn't get to use it? Providing enrichment activities allows the dog to use that fantastic brain. It allows them to affect outcomes and gives life a purpose.

The Five Elements of Canine Enrichment

The five main elements of canine enrichment are; Safe Environments, Food Enrichment, Non-Food Enrichment, Natural Behaviours and Companionship & Bonding. These elements never stand alone; there is always some degree of overlap between them. For example, food enrichment may also be acting on the need to perform natural behaviours, such as chewing or sniffing. The non-food enrichment of playing with a tug toy may also be providing companionship and building bonds. So why bother separating them into different elements, I hear you ask? Because this allows us to consider all of the dog's enrichment needs rather than concentrating on just one aspect and neglecting others.

It would be easy to think that enriching our dog's life was all about food. It's easy to think this because there are so many enrichment ideas based on feeding the dog in more interesting ways. It might be easy to fall into a pattern of just chucking the dog a Kong (rubber food stuffing toy) and thinking 'job done, my dog is enriched'. We might then miss out on a huge amount of other opportunities to bring a better life to our dogs. It's easy to think that food is the beginning, middle and end of enrichment. But what about the dogs who aren't massively food orientated? I've written many posts on social media about food enrichment and quite regularly somebody will comment, 'my dog's not interested in working for food'. On the one hand, as we'll discuss later, this can usually be rectified to some degree. On the other hand, we simply must appreciate that all dogs are not the same. Many Border Collies would be quite irritated by being offered food while they are engaged in the serious business of herding. Small dogs can often be far less 'foodie' than larger dogs. I'm not sure that I've fully convinced my Labrador, Mr B., but there really is more to life than food.

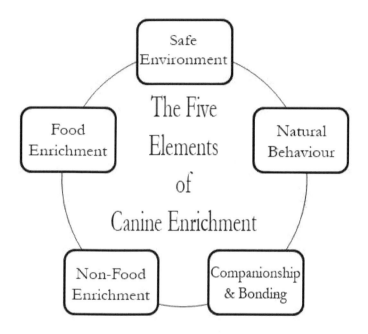

The Five Elements of Canine Enrichment

- Safe Environment
- Food Enrichment
- Natural Behaviour
- Non-Food Enrichment
- Companionship & Bonding

Safe Environment

Back in my school days, I didn't really fit in. I didn't seem to be able to learn like the other kids did. I spent most of my time in primary school sitting in the corner, facing the wall and copying from a book. It didn't seem to matter that I wasn't able to read the words in the book; I still had to copy them. I wasn't permitted to have a pen. Because of my poor writing skills I was only permitted to write with a pencil. I was severely dyslexic. The world of words didn't make sense to me. I was also a little different in other ways too. One Christmas time, I was trusted to join the rest of the class in painting Christmas pictures to decorate the classroom. What could possibly go wrong? We were each presented with a poster size (A1) outline print of a Santa Claus, snowman, or Christmas tree. I was given a Santa Claus. I eagerly painted my picture and gave it to the teacher. The teacher screwed up my painting as she yelled,

"YOU HAVE WASTED THIS PAPER; YOU HAVE WASTED ALL THIS PAINT, STUPID BOY".

Apparently, it wasn't good to be different at Buckton Vale Primary in 1975, and I'd painted my Santa bright blue. I just didn't get it. I didn't understand why I couldn't do the things other children could do, or what was wrong with a blue Santa Claus. Secondary school was even worse. I was in the bottom class for every subject. The teachers had given up even trying to teach me and I'd given up trying to learn. My only focus was on wanting each day to be over. Having despised every single day of my school life, I left aged 15

13

without a single qualification and would have struggled to write my own address. I began to self educate in my early twenties, at least enough to get by, but I remained very conscious of my educational shortcomings.

At 45 years of age, having spent my life feeling an affinity with dogs and their behaviour, I began a foundation degree course (Canine Behaviour & Training) at Bishop Burton College. What the hell was I doing? How could I possibly complete a degree course? I graduated with distinction and was awarded the Ian McParland award for greatest personal achievement. I continued onto a BSc (Hons) degree course (Canine Behaviour Management) and received a First.

Why do I tell this very personal story in a book about enriching the lives of our dogs? Because it shows just how important it is to provide a suitable environment. The school environment was not right for me, it did more harm than good, but at college I thrived. I was still a pain in the bum and slightly needy, but I thrived. Like never before, I thrived. It's difficult to put into words, but I feel like Bishop Burton College set me free.

What do dogs most need from their environment? They need to feel safe. A dog cannot enjoy an unsafe environment, or at least one that feels unsafe. Imagine having the dog's favourite enrichment toy on the lawn, stuffed full of his favourite food. The only problem is that the neighbours are letting off fireworks. Is the dog going to enjoy his food toy? It's highly unlikely. This is a fairly obvious observation. Most of us can understand that the dog doesn't feel safe. But how about when you go for a walk and bump into a strange dog, or there's lots of traffic, or you attend a new training class? Is it so easy to spot that the dog may be afraid or anxious in these situations?

Humans ask a lot from dogs. We often expect them to do just as we say, when we say it, no matter what. But do we stop to consider what the dog's needs might be? If we want the best *from* our dog and the best *for* our dog then we absolutely must consider their needs. And their overwhelming need is for a safe environment. Not one that merely seems safe to us, but one where the dog feels safe. It doesn't matter that we know the other dogs in an unfamiliar training class are safe; the dog needs to know it. I'm not suggesting we wrap dogs in cotton wool to protect them from the realities of life. Small amounts of stressful stimuli are necessary for developing the ability to cope when things go wrong. But life has plenty of natural stressors. For dogs living in a human world there are more than enough stressors. We don't need to be adding to them, we need to be reducing them.

We need to use the environment more. It's a rich source of enrichment opportunity. But, if the dog is fearful then the experience will not be enriching. Always remember that enrichment activities are not enriching merely because us humans think they should be. Enrichment is only enrichment if the dog finds it enriching. So get out there into the environment. Explore woodlands, moors, beaches, and parks. Find places where dogs can run free and explore and take in all the amazing scents. But do it at the dog's pace. Don't force them into situations they are not comfortable with.

Food Enrichment

Food enrichment is an exceptional tool. Food provides infinite opportunities for us to enrich our dogs. There are arguments against it (which we will discuss later) but for me, it's a gift from nature. The vast majority of living creatures spend a huge amount of time and energy on the acquisition of food. Evolution has produced animals which are highly motivated to find food. For any of us to be alive today, each of our ancestors, since life on earth began, has had to overcome the problem of acquiring enough nutrients to stay alive, at least long enough to reproduce. The unsuccessful ones didn't reproduce. This gives us millions of years worth of successful ancestors who were sufficiently motivated to find food. I've often heard people voice the concern that getting dogs to work for their food, via enrichment toys and activities, is cruel. But honestly, I'd feel cruel if I didn't feed my dogs in interesting ways. Believe it or not, dogs prefer the seeking to the finding of food. Dopamine (a neurotransmitter associated with rewarding experiences and pleasure) rises and peaks during the seeking, anticipation or wanting of something, not in the actual getting of the appetitive in question. Why would it be more rewarding for animals to seek than to actually get the thing they are seeking? The answer, of course, is that seeking requires far greater effort. If animals don't put in this effort, they will be unlikely to survive. Almost all animals on earth are the beneficiaries of a good work ethic. If seeking is more thrilling than finding and consuming, it would be easy to think that the finding doesn't really matter. But that most certainly isn't the case. The dopamine rush comes from the animal knowing that food might be available and having the opportunity to try and access it. If the food (or any other highly desired item for that matter) was never actually accessible then the animal would eventually lose interest. If there is no hope of success, there is no point in making the effort. There is no thrill of the chase if you don't get at least the occasional win. Evolution has shaped animals into hundreds of thousands of different forms, but none have evolved to do nothing all day and then have their food plonked in front of them in a bowl.

We don't have to ditch the food bowls completely. Many people who feed a raw meat diet are concerned about the prospect of not using a bowl. Rightly so, they need to be more careful about food hygiene and the risk of contaminating other surfaces and objects. It's slightly more challenging to do food enrichment with raw meat but it's certainly not beyond the human mind to come up with more interesting ways to offer it. I don't feed raw meat. I don't advocate feeding raw meat. But it seems to be growing in popularity so I discuss it here only because I don't want it to be a block to food enrichment. You may also be feeding other types of messy wet food and can't bear the thought of it getting on your best rug. If you want to continue feeding from a bowl then you can. Buy more bowls, buy 10 plastic bowls and hide them around the house and garden with a little food in each. The dog will have a great time seeking them all out. Always count the bowls when collecting them up. You don't want food left out to go rotten or attract flies. You will also need to be ultra careful if you have children around or if there are potential food guarding issues. Remember, our responsibility is to safeguard the dog and everyone around them, not to put them in a difficult or dangerous situation.

There are literally thousands of ways to use a dog's food for enrichment. I could write a book the size of War & Peace and still not catalogue them all. We can use food as it is but make it come alive, for example, rolling pieces of kibble across the kitchen floor. We can add it to a slow feeder (a cross between a maze and a bowl). We can stuff it in an enrichment toy, such as a Kong. We can hide it around the house for a treasure hunt. We can place it in empty cereal boxes, we can wrap it in a towel. We can hide it in puzzle feeders. We can use enrichment balls that dispense food as the dog pushes them around. Each of these examples has many different incarnations, seemingly limited only by our power of creativity.

Some people make up all sorts of fancy recipes to feed to their dogs. I'm not one of them. 90% of what my dogs eat is their normal daily diet. The other 10% is a few treats to make life interesting. Perhaps a few slivers of salmon or a small piece of chicken. I sometimes cut a slice of cheese into tiny (I mean tiny) cubes. I often give vegetables, mainly carrots, but these are extremely low in calories so hardly count. What we must avoid at all costs is overfeeding. A huge number of companion dogs are overweight. We absolutely must not add to this problem in the name of enrichment. Enrichment feeding is never about feeding extra calories. It's about feeding their main diet in more interesting ways.

If we are doing all sorts of food enrichment, how do we keep track of what they are eating? Work out how much of whatever you're feeding, your dog needs. Weigh it out each morning into a container. You can then use this as your supply throughout the day. How I do it: I weigh the food

18

into a container. I use about a third for activities in the morning, usually something simple, like scatter feeding. I use a third throughout the day for various activities, maybe a treasure hunt or maybe flicking the kibble across the floor for them to chase. The remaining third is kept for stuffing into food toys for the evening. When my family sit down to eat, the dogs get their food filled toys. This prevents dogs from scrounging or becoming anxious because there's food around. I'm going to labour the point, but it really is important to weigh the dog's food. When advising on behavioural issues, I often ask people to show me how much they feed their dog. They can be a little surprised when I whip out my weighing scales and compare the weight with the manufacturer's feeding guide. They are usually equally surprised to find out that they're overfeeding, often by a huge amount. If you don't weigh it, you don't know how much you're feeding.

There are a couple of drawbacks to the wonderful world of food enrichment. Some individual dogs just don't seem too keen to work for their food or they have poor appetites. Others can become obsessive over food to the extent that they seem uninterested in anything else. Some may display resource guarding issues, although resource guarding can also be a problem around other (non-food) items. Let's look at each.

The dog's not a foodie: In dog training circles, it's not uncommon to hear, 'my dog isn't motivated by food'. It's also not uncommon to hear the reply; 'if they weren't motivated by food they would be dead'. The reply may be true. For living things to stay living they must be motivated by food, at least enough to conduct the required movement of getting food from the outside to the inside. But the clever answer doesn't really help the dog's human companion. Their dog may still be far less motivated by food than the average dog. Or we may have selectively bred dogs to be very highly focused on other things. I often hear Border Collie guardians comment that their dog isn't much bothered about food. Many very small dogs are often not so motivated by food. Can you imagine how little food some of the tiny breeds actually need? A few special treats can often create very fussy eaters within small breeds. It seems logical that if you need less food than most other dogs, you can also afford to be fussier than most other dogs.

With dogs who are less food motivated, it's even more important to know how much you're feeding. Be very careful with adding little extras and make the food come alive. It's not a case of forcing the dog, against their will, to work for food. It doesn't have to take a great effort. We need to keep it simple yet exciting. Flicking a piece of kibble across a smooth kitchen floor has enticed many a dog to chase and eat it in situations where they wouldn't eat it from their bowl. Don't make it difficult, make it exciting. If you are concerned about your dog's appetite, you should always consult with a registered vet to rule out illness and disease. This is a very real possibility and should not be ignored.

The food obsessive: Using food for enrichment and training is something I very much advocate. But if everything we do with the dog relates to food we can sometimes produce dogs who are obsessed with looking for where the next morsel is coming from. They can become so keen for the expected food that they lose the ability to concentrate on anything else. A similar phenomenon is sometimes seen when we use very high value training treats, for example, fresh chicken. They can't think about anything other than the chicken, so the ability to learn is blocked. We can help by reducing the reinforcement value of the food, perhaps using kibble rather than chicken. We can introduce other forms of enrichment. Make sure life isn't just about food. Play tug, throw a squeaky toy, do some belly rubs, find some interesting scents, mix it up. Fantastic as it is, don't let the only enjoyment in life be food.

The resource guarders: Management of the environment is critical in resolving many dog behavioural issues. The aim is to prevent the behaviour problem from occurring whilst retraining progresses. In the case of food guarding, we can't very well stop feeding the dog. Instead, we ensure they eat only in a place of safety or at a distance from us where they do not feel the need to resource guard. Food enrichment can still be a suitable option for resource guarders, but extreme care should be taken as even when a food toy becomes empty the dog my still regard it as a highly prized resource. I highly recommend working with a suitably qualified canine behaviourist for any resource guarding issues. I include a general overview to my approach to working with resource guarding only to demonstrate the type of approach you should expect from a qualified behaviourist. My approach is as follows:

Imagine there's a stress zone around your dog when they have items to guard. When you step into the zone, the dog becomes stressed, possibly eating faster, freezing (or going very still), growling, showing the whites of his eyes (whale eye) or snapping. The zone might be 30 cm or it might be 10 metres and it might change depending on who steps into the zone and what is being guarded.

Now, every time you go near the zone (but not into it), reward the dog with a fantastic treat (maybe a cheese cube or slice of hotdog). The idea is that the dog begins to associate you approaching as the best thing in the world because he gets the cheese (or whatever) and keeps the item which was (or could be) being guarded, and you never enter the stress zone. Over time, and I'm talking months, NOT A FEW DAYS, the stress zone may reduce (allowing for you to move closer inch by inch) because the dog's stress of you approaching is reducing (if he's reacting you have gone too far/fast, take a step back). It's best to begin the process when the dog has lower value items and then repeat from the beginning with higher value items. It should also be done with each household member from the beginning. Don't assume that because the dog is happy for you to approach that he is happy for everyone else to approach, he might not be.

It's not magic. All dogs, humans, relationships, environments and situations are different. Some dogs will always retain a strong instinct to protect anything in their possession, especially if the behaviour has been ongoing for a long period of time.

Hitting, shouting, intimidating or being agonistic toward the dog in any way isn't likely to improve his anxiety of people getting too close. I think it's fair to say that it could make him more anxious. Additionally, punishing him for growling may teach him not to growl, the anxiety is still there but it's not so easily recognised, making it easier for people to get too close without realising the dog's stressful state. That may well result in a bite.

Every dog and human is different. This is a brief overview of my approach to resource guarding. It is NOT a set of instructions for curing every dog's guarding issues. I don't know your dog or your situation. You should employ a suitably qualified behaviourist to assess your situation and provide an appropriate behaviour modification plan.

I strongly believe that food can help provide enrichment for any dog. But it doesn't matter what I think. If you feel that it's not for you or your dog I can fully respect that. Enriching the dog should also make us humans feel good. If it doesn't then the appeal will soon fade. If we're not comfortable with any particular aspect or activity we can simply concentrate on the others.

Non-Food Enrichment

Non-food enrichment overlaps with all the other elements of enrichment, other than food. More specifically it's about dog toys, such as tugs, chew toys, rubber rings, squeaky toys, balls, knotted ropes, soft toys and fetching items. Overlapping with environmental, it can also include some excellent outdoor activities such as swimming and paddling. Additionally, there are many dog sports and activities that you can both get involved in, for example, agility, flyball, disc dog, and dock jumping. In recent years Rally-O and Canicross have become popular activities. Rally-O is a less formal obedience type competition where competitors walk the course and follow sign-posted instructions as they go. Canicross is a little more physically demanding. It's akin to cross country running with your dog.

These activities are not for everyone, many of us live busy lives. We need to be realistic otherwise we will not continue. Non-food toys often sit in a toy box unused. I've heard countless people comment that they've bought this, that and the other for their dog and they are just not interested in them. For a dog the novelty of a new toy can soon wear off. The toy has no food to deliver and it probably doesn't do very much; it doesn't chase or wiggle or try to escape. Watch two dogs playing and notice how much interaction is going on. It's like a dance, each dog responding to the movements of the other. Compare that with one dog playing with a toy. There's no real interaction, what's even meant to happen? Why would they continue to be stimulated? We must always be careful not to assume all dogs are the same. They are not. There certainly are some dogs who will manage to entertain themselves for hours with a few inanimate toys, but in my experience, many dogs soon begin to ignore them. Interestingly, these toys are often brightly coloured, yet a dog's colour vision is not the same as it is for humans. Dogs see yellow and blue, but not red or green. A bright red toy sitting on the lawn is something most humans will instantly spot, but for dogs it's just a dark muddy colour of little significance. These toys are often designed to appeal to humans. That's not entirely as illogical as it seems. If these items didn't appeal to humans as they browsed the shelves, the manufacturers would soon be out of business. Not many dogs get to choose their own things.

That's not the end of the story. These inanimate colourful toys which dogs often find boring are not at all useless. On the contrary, they're a fantastic opportunity for life not to be all about food. We just need to bring them to life. Imagine you have two knotted rope toys. Grab one and start engaging the dog, wiggle it around, drag it along the floor, let the dog pounce on it, have a gentle tussle, let the dog win it. Then grab the second rope toy and bring it to life in the same way. Throw it a little way for the dog to chase. Take hold of the first rope and start wiggling it. Get the dog excited about these toys and the interaction with you. If you did this for just five minutes each evening you would hugely improve your dog's enjoyment of life.

Natural Behaviours

By law, in the United Kingdom (and in many other countries around the world), companion and farm animals must be permitted to perform natural, species specific, behaviour. The Farm Animal Welfare Council developed what is known as The Five Freedoms to safeguard the welfare of animals. These are:

- FREEDOM FROM HUNGER AND THIRST

- FREEDOM FROM DISCOMFORT

- FREEDOM FROM PAIN, INJURY OR DISEASE

- FREEDOM TO EXPRESS NORMAL SPECIES SPECIFIC BEHAVIOUR

- FREEDOM FROM FEAR AND DISTRESS

In law they are regarded as needs rather than freedoms and cover all domesticated animals and wild animals living under human control. Animals are instinctively driven to perform innate behaviours. They don't operate independently though, they are still influenced, to some degree, by the environment.

In 1961 the Brelands (forerunners in animal training techniques) reported problems they were having when training pigs to place a wooden coin into a piggy-bank. Each time they successfully trained a pig to perform the trick they later ran into difficulties. Successively, the pigs, rather than carrying the coin straight to the piggy-bank as trained, would start rooting it into the ground. The Brelands were no amateurs. Dr. Sophia Yin described them as the best animal trainers in history and she is probably not wrong.

Even in the hands of the best animal trainers in history, the natural behaviour for pigs to root couldn't be denied. This phenomenon became known as instinctive drift: the tendency of a trained behaviour to drift towards an instinctive behaviour. Pigs root. It's what they do; it's what they are compelled to do. But what about dogs? What do dogs do?

Above all else, dogs sniff. They sniff everything. They don't care too much about how things look, that's a human thing, they care about how things smell. The scenting ability of dogs has been employed in various aspects, including explosive detection, fire-scene investigation, drug detection, finding missing persons, medical alert, hunting, and even identifying the presence of wood rot in telegraph poles.

Dogs use scent to inform them of the world around them, for example, whether an object is edible, recognising family members or dog friends, where to pee, another dog's gender, another dog's breeding status, recognising water, what other dogs are living in the neighbourhood, if an area is safe or if they've met somebody before. There are many examples of dogs who, for one reason or another, have not seen their main human companion for a long time. When they are reintroduced, the dog is often wary until they get close enough to inhale the person's scent. Then they go crazy with excitement. Scent is what tells them who this is; scent is how they interpret the world.

Studies have shown that when dogs sniff a novel odour they predominantly inhale via the right nostril. Providing the odour is associated with safety, the dog switches to the left nostril when presented with the odour again. If the novel odour is associated with something the dog finds aversive, for example, the scent of a particular veterinarian, then the switch doesn't take place. Scent receptors are known to serve the ipsilateral side of the brain which results in scents detected on the right hand side being processed in the right hand side of the brain. That right hemisphere of the brain is responsible for activating the hypothalamic-pituitary-adrenal axis, triggering the flight or fight response. Scent is clearly being used to indicate safety and danger.

Despite the number of uses we've found for the dog's scenting ability and all we know about how olfaction is used, when it comes to companion dogs, we largely ignore it. This is because humans, like all primates, are microsomatic. This means we have an underdeveloped sense of smell compared to most other mammals. Man and dog get along extremely well. We may be the most successful interspecific partnership ever. But our primary senses are different. The human umwelt is largely about aesthetics; the canine umwelt is largely about scent.

A dog's most common natural behaviour is sniffing. To walk a dog without allowing them to sniff is akin to taking children to the circus and not allowing them to watch. If I could choose only one enrichment activity to improve a dog's life it would be allowing them to stop and sniff. It's not just about letting them sniff, it's about allowing them to be a dog.

Another natural behavioural need is socialisation. It's a superb thing for a dog to have dog friends. To see dogs playing and chasing one another is a glorious thing. It's also very good physical exercise. Sociable dogs get huge benefits from meeting up with other compatible dogs. It's immensely enriching. However, many dogs don't get along with others so well. For these dogs it would not be enriching, it would be stress inducing. This isn't because it's not a natural behaviour, it may be because they've been raised without meeting compatible dogs during their early years (lack of appropriate socialisation), or they were frightened by a particular incident. Sometimes dogs are just not compatible. Some are too boisterous, intact males can be socially competitive. It's easy to think that if we do everything right our dog will have a friendly disposition. But life is seldom so easy. Things go wrong and behaviour is complex. Many good dog trainers have less than perfectly behaved dogs. We must face the fact that some dogs just don't get along. Keeping them safe is our first priority. If you know dogs that your dog gets along with, maybe arrange times to meet up in a place of safety.

Fortunately for us, dogs bond well with humans. Many even prefer humans to dogs. This may allow us to fulfil some of their social needs ourselves. Interact with them often. It sounds obvious that we'd interact with them often. But the reality of our busy modern lives can soon see them sliding down the list of priorities. A dog in a busy household can easily become a lonely dog. Ensure you are interacting, talking to them, petting them, playing with them and appreciating them.

A great number of dogs never get the opportunity to run free. It's understandable. If you're worried about them getting into trouble, their safety or their recall, you might want to keep them safely on lead at your side. Some breeds are legally prevented from being off lead in a public place. The ability to run is undoubtedly a natural and beneficial behaviour for dogs. If you can't allow it for safety or legal reasons, you may be able to hire a secure field or enclosure for an hour so your dog gets the opportunity to stretch their legs. If your dog is reactive to other dogs, it can often be that they're anxious, rather than aggressive. Consider working with a qualified behaviourist to help your dog feel more comfortable around other dogs. Recall is one of the most common problems I hear about. You let the dog have a good run around on the local field but when it's time to go home the dog plays hard to get. Actually, it's one of my favourite things to teach. As a guide, my general approach is as follows:

Recall: The dog (let's name him Fido) may have already learned to ignore the sound of your voice when you recall him outdoors. I suggest teaching him to come to the sound of a whistle; I use a gun-dog whistle (Acme Dog 211.5) because it's a nice sound and a good tone for dogs. Where the following instructions call for a treat to be given, use a small piece of chicken, a slice of hotdog or something else which they really enjoy. Food treats should be approximately the size of a fingernail to allow for lots of training without the dog overeating or getting bored with the food. Food treats could also be replaced by a favourite toy for some dogs (common with Border Collies).

When should you move from one step to another?

If Fido is responding well at least 4 out of 5 times you may proceed to the next step.

If Fido is responding well 3 out of 5 times, repeat the step.

If Fido is responding well less than 3 out of 5 times, go back to the previous step.

Step 1: With Fido nearby (indoors), blow the whistle and give a treat. Repeat 15 times per day for three days.

Step 2: Within the home and with Fido further away from you, perhaps the other side of the room, blow the whistle and give a treat as soon as Fido reaches you. Repeat 10 times per day for three days.

Step 3: Within the home and with Fido in another room from you, blow the whistle and give a treat as soon as Fido reaches you. Repeat 10 times per day for three days.

Step 4: Within the garden, blow the whistle and give a treat as soon as Fido reaches you. Repeat 10 times per day for three days.

Step 5: In a safe area outside of the home, and with Fido still on the lead, blow the whistle and give a treat. Repeat 5 times per day for three days.

Step 6: Within the safe area, remove the lead and allow Fido to have a run-around for five minutes before you begin training. Continue with Fido running free (as long as it is safe to do so) but each time he comes within five paces blow the whistle and give a treat. Immediately allow Fido to continue running free. Repeat 10 to 15 times for three days.

This step may be completed with a long line attached if you do not have a very safe area.

Step 7: Over the next 10 (approximately) training sessions repeat the instructions for step six but gradually increase Fido's distance from you when you blow the whistle. So you may increase the distance by five paces per training session.

Step 8: Repeat steps six and seven with added distractions (this will be easier to do with the help of a friend and their dog). Maybe a dog on the other side of the field which is far enough away as to not distract him too much.

Step 9: Repeat steps six and seven but increase the distractions slightly. Perhaps a little nearer to the distraction.

Step 10: Continue to add distractions in small increments. Perhaps getting closer to them or even playing with another dog if appropriate. If you advance to the level of recalling when playing, then it's best to wait for a pause in the play, otherwise, he may not even notice the whistle if he is in full flow.

Step 11: Continue to practice in other safe areas where you may want to let Fido off lead. New areas should first be practised without the added distractions.

Note: The reason Fido comes to you when you blow the whistle is that he gets a treat and is also permitted to continue to play. This behaviour should be maintained by regularly blowing the whistle during off lead time, giving a treat and allowing Fido to go and play again. On any occasion when you need to put Fido back on the lead, give him a few treats after he's securely attached. This will help to ensure that he is always happy to go back on the lead.

The advantage to using a whistle is that it is very distinctive. The disadvantage is that you may leave home without it. I always keep one on my keyring. However, the very same process can be done using a distinctive word or sound. I often use a 'WUB' sound, just because it's distinctive and can cut across other noises.

Companionship & Bonding

Dogs are highly sociable animals. They don't tend to do well in isolation. One of the main reasons that dogs often struggle to cope in rehoming kennels is that it's difficult for the staff to give each dog enough human contact. Dogs just enjoy hanging out with us and our lives are all the richer for it. We bred them this way. Dogs are one of few animals which play as adults. We bred this too. We love puppies, we can't help ourselves. We're hugely attracted to puppy features and so this is what we've selected for over thousands of years. It may often have been subconsciously, but nevertheless, we've produced dogs which remain infantile their whole lives, or at least into their twilight years. In many respects, dogs are like children which never grow up. Of course, they are not all playful. Some don't play. But this is more likely a symptom of how they've been treated in the past or a symptom of pain or discomfort. Not all breeds or individuals are the same. Indeed, all things in nature are variable so we should avoid drawing hard and fast rules. But dogs don't grow up and leave home or ever have to fend for themselves. They remain totally dependent on us. It's not surprising then that they can become stressed when isolated in kennels or during the long periods that humans may have to work.

Companion dogs crave the safety of their family unit. I usually recommend that people have two dogs rather than just one. This allows them to speak their own language, play, sniff and feel less isolated when we are not around. Countless times, I've sat watching the dogs play together and wondered, how did I ever have just one dog? But it's not possible for everyone to have more dogs and it's not always suitable. Some dogs do better on their own and if you have socially competitive dogs where squabbles break out then they would need separating at times when we are not there to supervise. Even when dogs get along perfectly well, they're still very much in need of human company. General opinion seems to be that they shouldn't be left any longer than four hours. But all dogs are different; some cannot be left for a few minutes without becoming stressed. In reality, it's clear that many dogs are left for over eight hours whilst their human goes to work. Most enrichment products are sold under the instruction that the dog should be supervised whilst using it. Obviously there are safety risks to having dogs active when we are out. If their jaw gets stuck around a toy or they swallow something they shouldn't, we won't be there to help. We must always weigh up the risk. I think it's far better to teach dogs to settle when the human leaves. This should be their down time, not their active time. If you absolutely must leave dogs for long periods while you work, think about getting somebody to come in and see them for an hour, or perhaps employ a dog walker. I know! It costs money and it's not going to be affordable for everyone. And that's the stark reality! Many dogs will be left for long hours. All the more reason to ensure the time we do get to spend with them is quality time.

The best way for us to bond with our dogs and allow them to feel that they truly belong, is by doing things with them. Interact with them, sit on the floor with them, play with them, gently stroke them as you watch television. Above all, let them feel safe in your company. We don't need to yell at dogs. How easily do they hear the clink of their lead as you pick it up to take them out? Why would we need to yell? We don't need to be harsh with dogs at all. This only makes them feel unsafe and produces behaviour problems. Good relationships are built on trust. For a dog to truly bond with us and feel safe, they simply must be able to trust that we won't hurt them.

The human half of the partnership is the one who usually gets to choose things. We choose the dog's diet, time of feeding, when to go for a walk, where to walk, training instructor, enrichment activities, vet and just about everything else. There's obviously good reason for us to be the choice maker but we need to let the dog make some choices too. We need to take notice of when the dog is saying 'I'm not comfortable with that, I don't want to do it'.

If we pick up a puppy and they struggle, our impulse is often to hold the puppy more tightly. The pup's instinct may be to try harder to escape. In actual fact, if we were to put the puppy back down at the first hint of a wriggle he would learn that to get down he only needs to give a slight wriggle. In the long run, the ability to get down when he wishes is more likely to make him happy to be picked up. Contrast this with the dog who is tightly held on to; he may become very averse to being picked up because he knows there is no way out; he doesn't have a choice. This is exactly how behaviour problems arise. The puppy may learn that the only way to prevent being picked up is to bite or run away. If we give animals more choice we're more likely to get the behaviour we want and a better relationship will come along for the ride. When we give animals a choice, something special happens, they learn to trust us.

Introducing Enrichment Activities

The introduction of new activities can sometimes be daunting for dogs. They don't always instinctively know what to do. Some will enthusiastically jump straight into exploring a new item. But, depending on the activity, even these dogs are not always successful. In dog training, we don't try to teach a complex behaviour all in one go and expect the dog to understand. The first step in training a dog to stay in the down position, whilst the handler goes to the opposite side of the training hall, wouldn't be to say, "down", and walk away. We'd need to teach a 'down'. We might then teach that it's a good thing to stay there for a few seconds by giving treats. We might then introduce a release cue, then build duration, then slowly increase distance. And if we're really doing a proper job, we'd have made sure the dog is comfortable in this environment and we'd practice at home where there are fewer distractions. In short, we take baby steps. Enrichment should be no different. We need to start off simple and ensure the dog is successful.

What the Dog Wants: There are hundreds, if not thousands, of dog enrichment toys on the market, from the classic Kong, to newcomers, like the Pickpocket Foragers. There are many other activities we can provide without buying a thing. One of the most common is to use old food boxes. It's quick, simple, and free. It usually involves placing the dog's food into the box and letting the dog have a great time ripping the box up to get the food out. It's one of my favourite things to do. However, we must evaluate safety risks. All enrichment should be supervised, but with DIY enrichment there are some greater risks to consider. Are the materials dog safe? Will the dog consume things they shouldn't? If your dog would eat the cardboard then this type of activity shouldn't be done. At least not until the dog has learned not to eat cardboard. Other risks with cardboard, might be the glue used in manufacturing or even large staples in some of the larger cardboard boxes. I love boxes. My dogs love boxes. But they will not be safe for every dog. Always evaluate the possible risks for you, your dog and your situation, especially for DIY enrichment.

In a review of enrichment studies on captive animals, Wells (2009) found that the type of enrichment which gave the greatest benefit were activities which promoted the use of the animal's dominant sense. With our dogs, this is most definitely the sense of smell. All dog breeds, including sight hounds, have a stunningly brilliant sense of smell which they use constantly to gather information about the world around them. But dogs do differ. No other species on earth exists in such varying phenotypes. By selectively breeding dogs for particular uses, we've produced different breeds with varying innate behaviours. Considering the breed's original use can give us clues toward which types of enrichment activity they may prefer. However, dogs are individuals and not all dogs of the same breed will enjoy the same things. Labradors are known for their love of water but not every individual within the breed will be a water lover. We must get to know our own individual dog and what rocks their world.

Enrichment Activities

(but not always)

This is the most challenging section of the book to write. There are just so many activities to choose from. I've chosen activities which are reasonably easy for us to provide. I like to keep things relatively simple. The activities should also be enjoyable for us. Realistically, if they aren't easy to provide or enjoyable, most of us will not keep up with them.

Please remember two very important things as you read through the activities:

1: Not all dogs enjoy the same things.

2: There is always a risk to be considered.

When you step out of your front door in the morning, there's a risk. It's a reasonably low risk, but you could trip on the step and break your ankle. When you cross the road the risk increases, but it's still quite low for most of us. For children and the elderly the risk is considerably higher. If we choose to remain safely indoors we're still at risk, because it's actually where most accidents occur. We can't live totally risk free. But nor should we be blasé about it. We must constantly evaluate the risks for our dogs. For example, if your dog is partial to eating non-food items (pica) then you should take all precautions to avoid access to the non-food items. Activities such as ripping open a cereal box wouldn't be appropriate. I also discuss some popular choices which I don't believe to be hugely enriching. It's not enrichment just because humans call it enrichment; the dog has to think so too. I've purposely avoided simply making a list of products. This section is more about how to use different types of enrichment rather than being a comprehensive list of what is available.

Wiggle & Tug: Take two similar tug toys and hold them behind your back. Bring one to life, wiggling it and dragging it in front of the dog. Have a short gentle game of tug. Then stop tugging and bring the second toy into action, wiggling it around and getting the dog to engage for a quick game. Then stop with that one and bring the first back to life. The dog will almost always be interested in the object you bring to life and make interesting. As you play this game, swapping between toys, start to give a cue word which will indicate to the dog that you are going to swap to the other toy. The cue word could be anything you like but let's go with 'bananas' for now. Just as you stop playing with toy 'A' say "bananas" and produce toy 'B'. The dog learns to let go in order to start a new game with the other toy. On the final release, when you don't wish to continue playing, chuck something for the dog to chase so he doesn't learn that letting go means game over. Once learned, this skill of releasing on cue may enable the game to stop and restart or may be transferred to other games, such as the Flirt Pole.

Flirt Pole: What on earth is a flirt pole? It's basically a kind of baton or flexible cane with an elasticated cord. A toy or knotted fleece is attached to the end of the cord. Imagine a whip with something tied on the end and you won't be far wrong. The idea is to use the toy like a puppet on a string. By moving the baton, it's relatively easy to make the toy jump and dash around. Let the dog chase the toy but also let them catch it. We are not teasing the dog, we're giving them something to chase and catch. When they catch the toy, have a gentle game of tug for 5 or 10 seconds and start again. If you have difficulty getting the dog to release the toy so the game can restart there are a couple of strategies you can use.

1: You could have another toy ready to bring to life, maybe a squeaky one. Give a few squeaks and chuck it for the dog to chase. Give him a few seconds to enjoy his victory of getting it and then start the flirt pole game again.

2: You could give a little treat as a reward for catching the flirt pole toy, this way he lets go to get the treat. However, I'm not a big fan of using food during fast paced games. The dog often ends up coughing because he hadn't eaten the food properly, such was the rush to get playing again. Furthermore, these types of games do not usually require food reinforcement. The game is reinforcement enough and although I use food enrichment a lot, I don't want enrichment to be just about accessing food.

3: Add a cue word separately to get the dog to release. See the Wiggle & Tug activity for instructions on how to do this. The dog learns to let go in order to get you to restart the game.

When it's time to end the game you could give the dog something else, perhaps throwing a squeaky toy so that the game ends on a positive note rather than you just taking the flirt pole away.

Caution is necessary in regard to dogs taking fast, sharp turns which could result in injury. Growing puppies may be at particular risk because their joints are not yet fully formed. Be very gentle with puppies; they are babies, not miniature dogs.

Squeak & Chase: Take two squeaky toys. My preference is the Animal Instincts SkinFling range (see following image), as they are also fantastic for wiggle & tug activities. Give toy 'A' a few squeaks and get the dog interested, show the toy, and toss it a few metres away. Let the dog grab it and have a few seconds of glory in his victory. Now start squeaking toy 'B'. As soon as the dog turns his attention back to you (or the noise) toss the toy in the opposite direction to the first. You may retrieve toy 'A' whilst the dog is focussed on toy 'B' and repeat the process. This is not about trying to beat the dog to the toy. Only pick up a toy if the dog is fully focused on the other one or the game may turn into an altogether different one of each trying to grab the toy before the other. That's not what we want. We never want to encourage resource guarding. Never be tempted to tease the dog. We only need to be using the squeaker once or twice and then tossing the toy. Remember, we're there to please, never to tease. This game could be enjoyed by any dog but terriers seem to particularly love it. Probably because many were originally bred to hunt squeaky rodents

Scatter Feeding: Scatter feeding is the process of scattering the dog's food across the ground, like you might if you were feeding chickens. The dog gets to engage that fantastic olfactory system as he tracks down each individual piece of food. Scatter feeding can be done indoors, on the lawn, or when out and about. Short grass works well because it hides each food piece, increasing the need for engaging the nose to sniff them out. If your dogs are raw fed, then for hygiene reasons, this may not be suitable, but you may want to consider using dehydrated meat treats for scattering.

Scatter feeding has become relatively popular. It's easy to see why; it's quick, easy, and dogs love it. However, it's also attracted some criticisms. I recently read the comments of a dog trainer on social media. They considered that scatter feeding would teach dogs to eat anything they find and that this may ultimately kill them. We can't simply ignore such a concern without considering the risks.

Actually, the majority of dogs, given the opportunity, would eat food that they stumble across outdoors. A major factor in the process of domestication was the eagerness of dogs' ancestors to scavenge from around human settlements. Animals didn't evolve by sitting around waiting for food to come along and jump into their mouth. They took opportunities to eat wherever they arose. By nature, dogs are scavengers. Dogs need no encouragement to scavenge. But it's our responsibility as their guardians to do all we can to ensure they do not come into contact with harmful substances.

Could we be encouraging more scavenging by scatter feeding? Dogs are quite expert at reading our body language and learning cues. They tend to notice our every move. This isn't really surprising because we are the provider of all they want and need. If a dog has ever been fed scraps from the dinner plates, he'll eagerly follow you to the kitchen to see if he's getting anything. Right from the moment you began to move your foot to stand up, he was on to you, eager and keen. We don't need to formally train this. The dog has learned that your movements, in this context, indicate the possibility of a food treat. The same thing happens with scatter feeding. Just from our behaviour prior to scatter feeding, they learn that the game is on. It's possible that scatter feeding may decrease their likelihood to be looking for food items at other times because they have learned the predictors and this is when they go into seeking mode. We must still be cautious. We must be sure that the area we're scatter feeding in is free of pesticides or other harmful substances. There is also a potential risk which comes from ingesting snails or their slimy trails, which can transmit lungworm to dogs. Speak to your vet about lungworm risks in your area. If in doubt, reserve scatter feeding for the home environment, maybe on a deep pile rug or snuffle mat (see next activity).

Snuffle Mat: A Snuffle Mat consists of an abundance of fleece strips connected to rubber matting. The strips stick up from the matting and provide hundreds of hiding places for the dog's food. My preferred method of loading the mat is to scatter a handful of kibble (or other dry food) onto the top and then run my fingers gently through the mat to disperse the kibble deep into it. This exercise engages their olfactory senses and puts them into seeking mode. This tends to be a calming exercise too because the dog needs to concentrate. Dogs make it look easy but in reality, it's a tricky undertaking requiring great concentration. The mat is covered in the scent of the food, but the food can't be seen. As food moves or is eaten it leaves scent behind on the fleece. The dog needs to learn that only certain strength of odour is going to pay off and that the weaker strength odour is simply where food has been but is no longer.

Introducing the snuffle mat is usually straightforward but not all dogs will use it as expected straight away. Some, if they are not used to enrichment activities, may not engage with it. Others may pick it up and shake it. For dogs who don't engage with it you can start off with the mat on the floor and away from you. Give a few treats to the dog, drop a few on the floor, work your way closer to the mat, drop treats by the mat, then on top of the mat, and then you can start hiding them below fleece strips. If at any stage the dog becomes less keen, go back a step. It doesn't have to happen overnight, take your time, give them choices. For dogs who pick the mat up to play with, we need to ensure that the focus is on seeking the food rather than on the pure enjoyment of ruffing up a mat. Ensure that the food is clearly visible, maybe a pile of food next to the mat. Next time, maybe in a bowl sat on the mat, next, pile the food on top of the mat without a bowl, then start working some of it into the mat. You can do this over a few days, don't rush it. Once a dog has picked up a snuffle mat and food falls from it, they may learn that this is a quick way to access the food. It's not the end of the world, try retraining by making it easier to leave the mat in position (as suggested) or enjoy letting them be a smarty pants, the choice is yours. I recommend removing and storing the snuffle mat out of sight when not in use. I don't want them using it as a toy or a bed and items which sometimes contain food can easily become items to resource guard, even when empty of food. I don't know who originally came up with the idea of snuffle mats (that was probably not the original name for them as I've heard many alternative names) but I wish I did, because they're a game changer.

Cardboard Boxes: Do you place your used food boxes straight into the recycling? Why not use them for quick and easy enrichment for your dog? Light weight food packaging boxes are those which are used for cereals and many frozen foods. Place a few dog food items inside and give it to your dog. They're usually thrilled with the opportunity to rip into a cardboard box. They use scent to inform them of the prize. But they also get to use their paws and mouth in coordination to hold and rip open the box. When they get good at this game, you can put boxes inside boxes. The only downside to this fabulous fun activity is that cleaning up the cardboard is a solely human activity. Another option is to substitute the food for a favourite toy, or chew treat.

This isn't suitable for dogs who eat non-food items (pica) because they may eat the cardboard. You can work with a behaviourist to turn this around, but even then, it's probably not going to be an appropriate activity for your dog. I've been asked many times if it's okay for dogs to eat cardboard. The answer is no, absolutely not. Always supervise. Always consult your vet for advice if your dog eats any non-food item. Dogs shouldn't be chewing on the cardboard. They should only be ripping bits off to get inside.

People often use bigger boxes too. The sort that large goods are delivered in. With a bigger box comes a bigger risk factor. Some of these large boxes may have strong or excessive amounts of glue applied during the packaging processes and they are sometimes constructed using staples. Anecdotally, I've heard third-hand stories of dogs' mouths being glued shut because of the glue on boxes. With the risk of sounding repetitive, I'll say it again; we must always consider what risk any activity might have.

Activity Mat: There are a few activity mats around now but I think the first, at least the first which I remember, was the Buster Activity Mat. The padded, wipe clean, mat has press studs to allow different activities, from cone cloth to top hat, to be easily attached. It's a great toy to encourage investigating and promoting choices, because there are so many options, many of which are sold separately but are not too expensive.

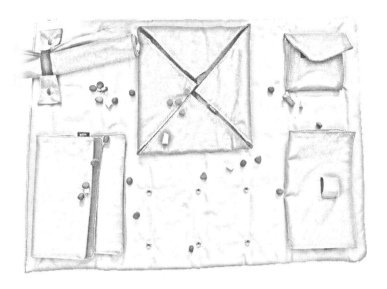

You will see your dog using his paws and neck muscles as he tries to navigate a route to the food. There are three levels of task difficulty. This shows knowledge on the part of the designer, dogs need to learn and start at an easy level. However, to start with, I'd just scatter food onto the mat and increase necessary engagement later. If you don't guide them in small incremental steps, they may try ripping the components as they would with a cereal box. Dogs are super smart but they don't know the difference between something you're going to chuck away in the recycling and a brand new activity mat that you want to keep. Despite popular opinion, I don't believe that dogs evolved to solve complex puzzles. They can learn complex sequences but we teach these step by step. For this reason, the Buster Mat is probably as puzzling as it gets for my dogs and for this book. Enrichment is a simple, organic process, not University Challenge.

Pickpocket Foragers: A relative newcomer to the canine enrichment market, Pickpocket Foragers are a large piece of fleece with shallow pockets covering the entire surface. The original can be used on the floor or hung on the side of a dog crate or gate. There are also other designs, such as the caterpillar. Food is placed inside some of the pockets and the dog gets to work finding it. The Pickpocket Foragers spark the dog's brain into seeking mode as they search for the hidden treasures within. Start off with the treats sticking out of the pockets (I used small gravy bone biscuits) then move on to laying them down, out of sight. Amazingly simple, yet highly engaging.

Kong Classic: Kong now make hundreds of enrichment products but the original, Kong Classic, remains one of my favourites. They're a bell shaped rubber toy which you stuff with food.

Wet food is best for this because dry food will pretty much just fall straight out. This is an activity where raw feeders can more easily participate, but as always, you'll need to be aware of possible contamination of the contact areas as food is released from the Kong. I'm not advocating raw feeding. Please discuss such matters with your vet and/or suitably qualified canine nutritionist. For kibble feeders, soak the kibble in a little water until soft and mushy. There are thousands of Kong stuffing recipes online if that's your thing, but I like to keep it simple. I often mix the kibble with chopped carrot and broccoli. Mix it all up and squish it into the Kong. Many people freeze the Kong to make them last longer but I tend to pack them tightly and place in the refrigerator. A frozen Kong may be making life just that little bit too difficult for many dogs. Kongs help to fulfil a dog's instinctive chewing behaviour. As the Kong is chewed, pieces of food loosen and fall out. However, some dogs learn an alternative method of dropping the Kong on the floor. A food stuffed Kong can be used to keep a dog happy and content while the human family eat their evening meal. To start off easy, put food in that can easily fall out. To increase the level of interaction needed, wrap the Kong in a towel.

K9 Connectables: These are bell and ball shaped capsules made of thermoplastic elastomer. Each can be filled with your dog's favourite food and clicked together to resemble something that wouldn't look out of place floating beside the International Space Station.

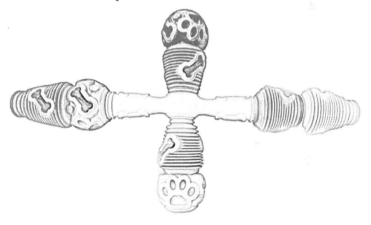

What's fabulous about these is that they are connected together to make one object but the dog then achieves great satisfaction from breaking them apart. Different skills are needed to break them apart and then access the food in the compartments. They even have little bone shaped holes in the sides where K9 Connectable treats fit into, very snuggly. The outside of the capsules are ridged in such a way that wet food can be smeared on. This gives an easy way of introducing them to dogs who are new to enrichment. They aren't sold as scent based enrichment but I've found that dogs are using the olfactory ability even here. If I connect ten capsules together and only some of them contain food, Mr B. will only separate the connections leading to the food filled capsules. He can only be using his sense of smell to do this. K9 Connectables can be frozen too, but as with Kongs, I don't tend to bother. If it's frozen, the dog will probably need to chew it harder to release the food. This will almost certainly result in a shorter product life. But if money is no object, freeze away. And maybe buy extra copies of my book as gifts for all your friends.

Licki Mat: Licki mats are thermoplastic elastomer mats, consisting of a grooved surface. Smear on wet food and let the dog get licking. They can also be frozen to make a cool treat on hot summer days. I often see the action of licking, described as soothing. This isn't necessarily the case because all behaviour is contextual. Dogs licking/cleaning one-another is usually done in a relaxed manner and appears to be soothing. In contrast, repetitive licking can also be an indicator of stress and poor welfare, as seen in the condition of acral lick dermatitis. Licki mats may have their uses but I'm not convinced they are highly enriching. To lick for twenty minutes to eat your food could just as likely be frustrating. There's no active seeking or scenting going on; it's just lick, lick, lick, lick, lick. All dogs are different and like different things, but I'd err on the side of caution and reserve licki mats for an occasional cool treat which last around 5 minutes. These mats are easily chewed and damaged. Ensure you are supervising (I advise supervising all enrichment) and that dogs do not get the opportunity to swallow pieces of the mat.

Sniffari: A sniffari is another way of thinking about your dog walk. Don't just take them for a walk; take them for a sniff. The saddest thing I see on a daily basis is people walking their dogs but not allowing them to stop and sniff. The human thinking is, 'we're going for a walk'. Dogs don't think, 'we're going for a walk'. The excitement you see when you pick up the lead isn't because the dog simply gets to walk. It's because the outside world is hugely stimulating. It's not the physical act of walking that excites them; it's the stimulation of an outside world, full of new scents. And what do we do when we take them outside into this rich world of scent. We walk, and if the dog stops to sniff, we pull them away, even chastise them. We chastise the dog for being a dog. I had to stop writing after that sentence and just ponder. I'd like you to stop too. Just stop and think about all the times we humans ask dogs not to be dogs.

Just as the bird was born to fly and the fish was born to swim, the dog was born to sniff. So don't think about taking dogs for a walk, think instead about taking them on a sniffari. Or if you don't like silly made up words, a sniff. Let them stop and take in their world. Let them sniff flowers, the grass, the scent left on your doorstep from a neighbour's cat, and dog pee left on every lamppost. Dogs are thought to be able to tell an awful lot from sniffing another dog's urine, particularly gender and breeding status. The synapses burst into life, transmitting information around the brain about who's in the neighbourhood. How is a dog to feel safe if he doesn't even know who else is around? If this book changes nothing else in your life, let it at least allow you to appreciate watching your dog stop and sniff. It's not a chore to stand waiting for the dog to stop sniffing; it's a privilege.

Search and Rescue: This is simply my favourite thing in the world. We're not looking for injured persons on Ben Nevis. But we can use the dog's phenomenal scent searching skills in a rather more comfortable setting. We're going to teach the dog to find a mouse. Not a real mouse. No enrichment for one species should come at the expense of stressing others. No, this is a toy mouse. I originally taught this game with one designed as a cat toy, but it's a little small so there is risk of them being accidentally swallowed. Try to get something bigger. You could use any soft dog toy for this but actually a face cloth tied in a knot might serve equally well. I'll continue to call it a mouse and if you don't tell the dog it's only a face cloth he'll never know. You'll also need to purchase a tub of dried catnip.

Step 1: Place some catnip in a tupperware container (enough to cover the bottom). Place kitchen roll (paper towel) over the catnip and place your mouse (or not a mouse) on top of the kitchen roll. Keep the lid on while stored. The mouse takes on the odour of the catnip and provides a distinctive scent for the dog to track.

Step 2: Using the mouse, play fetch with your dog, throwing the mouse just a short distance. If your dog doesn't fetch things back to you, no worries, you can just let him chase and grab the mouse. To get it back, have another toy to throw or switch to some scatter feeding with a few treats. Be careful not to chuck the mouse again until the dog has well and truly stopped eating for at least 10 seconds. If the dog is reliably fetching or at least chasing and picking up the item, you can tell him to 'Find It' whenever you throw the mouse. This will become the dog's signal to go and look for the item later in the process.

Step 3: Place the mouse instead of throwing it, and encourage the dog to 'Find It' (it helps if you have a good wait behaviour but it's not crucial). Reward with another toy, game or food.

Step 4: Start putting the mouse just out of sight but allow him to see where you put it (maybe in an open box).

Step 5: Place it in easy to find places but without him seeing where you put it

Step 6: Increase the difficulty by placing the item in more challenging places around the house or garden and telling him to 'Find it' If he has seen you get the mouse container he will certainly know that the game is on so will not be too dependent on the 'Find It' signal. It is nice to have the signal (cue) if you advance to hiding the mouse without his knowledge.

Always ensure the dog is competent and keen at each step and always play fair. Don't ever place it where he can't reasonably access it. This is extremely good brain exercise. You can see the concentration and focus as the dog uses scent, not just casually, but purposefully, to find a particular object. The dog is rewarded (or reinforced if we want to be technical) by the mere act of seeking (remember the dopamine rush). Further reinforcement comes from finding the item (if he was never able to find it he'd eventually give up trying) and further still from the game or food reinforcement we provide for him finding it. It's a bonanza of good stuff.

Plastic Cups: Take ten plastic cups or bowls, the kind which stack inside one-another. Place a few treats in each cup and stack them up. Place it on the floor for a quick and easy activity. This is real easy because the cups separate with little effort. But it builds confidence in manipulating objects and gives something interesting to do. Another quick and easy game with the cups is to turn each upside down on the floor with treats underneath. Start with treats under all of them, then reduce down to half. Some dogs will sniff to check whilst other will bash them all over.

Ten Bowls are Better than One: I spend a fair amount of my time encouraging people to ditch the dog bowl but that's not for everyone so maybe go the other way and buy ten dog bowls. That might be expensive so just use something cheap, like the containers fast food restaurants often use for deliveries. Put a little of their food in each container and hide them around the house and let them have fun finding them all. I'd start with just two or three in plain sight and work up from there. Always count the bowls afterwards so you don't have rotting food anywhere. You will need to be extra careful if you have children around or dogs which may guard their food.

Swimming: Swimming is great physical exercise but also mentally stimulating. Some breeds (like Labradors) have a love of water, but that doesn't mean each individual of the breed will love it. Finding themselves suddenly in deep water, isn't a choice and isn't enrichment. Start easy where it's shallow and the dog can choose to paddle or swim. We need to avoid stagnant water as lots of nasty things live there but we also need to avoid fast running water which could pose a risk, as well as very cold water or ice. There is also some degree of water toxicity risk in situations where the dog swallows too much water. As with many activities I like to keep them relatively short. Nobody wants a tired dog out in a body of water.

Live Streaming: This is as simple as finding a shallow stream and letting the dog have fun paddling and jumping in and out of the water. It's a natural and stimulating resource which dogs may not often come into contact with. It's great for dogs who love water but don't like, or have the confidence, to swim.

Woodland Friends Burrow: The Woodland friends burrow is toy made by ZippyPaws. It's basically three soft chipmunks (with squeakers inside) and a tree trunk. You get the dog interested in a chipmunk then put it in the tree trunk for the dog to retrieve. As always, take it in small steps to ensure success. The game isn't to rip up the tree trunk; it's to get the chipmunk out through the hole. Start by just sticking one third of the chipmunk in the hole and increase from there. I don't mention many brands in this book. That's because I didn't want it to be a collection of adverts, but a collection of ideas which can be expanded and explored. However, this toy surprised me. I didn't expect dogs to use it as designed. I thought they'd just treat it as one big soft toy, but they do seem to take great enjoyment out of retrieving the chipmunks from inside the tree stump. This game may particularly suit terrier type breeds, whose ancestors were often used for pulling small animals out of burrows and hiding places.

Shoes: A very simple way to use all those shoes you have sat at the bottom of a cupboard. Line them up side by side across the floor.

Hide treats in between the tightly packed shoes. As always, start easy with some treats visible. The dog gets to sniff and nudge his way along the shoes to find all the food. You may be thinking that this will encourage dogs to chew your shoes. Absolutely not. The dog is actually, more likely, learning that the stimulation doesn't come from the shoe but by investigating around them. Never put food into the shoe as this may encourage them to interact with it more than we want.

The Towel: Lay a towel out on the floor and sprinkle food over it. Roll it up and let the dog enjoy unrolling and finding all the treats. This is a really simple idea that I put online some years back. Now everyone's doing it. I must apologise to all the hoteliers out there because I've seen it used lots of times by people stuck in a hotel (with their dog) without any enrichment toys. There are many variations too, like, instead of rolling the towel, holding the middle and twisting it around so that it scrunches up into a kind of spiral shape.

Dogs use their nose for this task much more than you'd think.

Tea Towel Sandwich: Lay a tea towel on the floor and sprinkle with food, then simply lay another on top. This is trickier for the dog than you might think and a great alternative to the towel roll.

Marker Cones: Marker cones are used in sports training sessions. They're slightly smaller than a dinner plate and have a hole in the centre. They're very lightweight and easy to stack and store. They're also amazingly good for lining up and hiding treats underneath. I place 100 in the garden with treats under ten of them. The dog's job is to find the ten with treats inside. Start off simple, one cone, one treat. Then maybe two cones, one treat, all the way up to ten and increase it from there, adding a treat each time you start another ten. I first used these cones in a university research project to test the scenting ability across different breeds. Every shape, size, age, and breed were able to find food placed under the cones without any prior training or knowledge that there was food to be found. Yet another example that dogs need no training or encouragement in scavenging or foraging.

The Social Dog: Dogs make dogs' lives richer. To be able to socialise with your own species is an important aspect of being a dog. Dog socialisation is often neglected somewhat. We're often very protective of our dogs, not wanting them to mix with other dogs in case they get hurt or frightened. It's quite understandable. A bad experience, particularly in early life, can have long lasting consequences. But lack of experiences can also have long lasting consequences. If dogs don't socialise with other dogs they don't learn all the subtleties of canine body language. They don't get to fine tune their playing skills. When video of dogs playing is slowed down we see hundreds, if not thousands, of tiny actions and reactions as the two dogs interact in play. They almost never clash heads or get accidentally poked in the eye. Yet these are exactly the injuries you'd expect of young children playing so enthusiastically. Dog's reactions are superfast compared to ours. Socialisation is a tricky subject because we try to give dogs only pleasant experiences and avoid bad experiences. There are many very good puppy socialisation classes (there are also many awful ones) which match puppies' size, exuberance and competitiveness so that puppies don't become frightened or bullied. This can go a long way to helping dogs learn the skills they need in a protective environment. However, meeting other friendly dogs of equal disposition is not always the reality of life. Mr B. learnt from older dogs that not all dogs want to play with an exuberant young lab. That's not something I could teach him. Sure, I could teach him not to approach other dogs without my cue, but that would teach him to watch me rather than them. If dogs are to be able to socialise with other dogs, they need to learn dog social skills from other dogs. In our understandable desire to keep them safe we may have become too controlling. This can block their ability to learn appropriate interaction with other dogs. Some dogs are quite fussy with who they play with, but if you know some that your dog gets along well with, arrange a few weekly meet-ups for a good play session. It's not going to be appropriate for all dogs; many have already developed social issues, but if your dog is able to play with others, don't let them miss out on this irreplaceable life enriching behaviour. If you have young dogs, get them out into the world and socialise them with other sociable dogs. They won't learn social skills sat indoors.

59

I see frequent posts on social media from dog guardians and trainers, outraged at others allowing a dog to approach their dog without permission. Often it's because their dog is frightened or reactive, or that the other dog is too boisterous. These issues are largely due to a lack of appropriate socialisation in early life.

Kong Wobbler: The wobbler is a pear-shaped treat dispenser which is weighted at the bottom in such a way that it always rights itself no matter what position the dog puts it in. There's one hole in the side where treats fall out as the dog knocks it around. These seem incredibly strong. I've used the same one for years and it's still going strong. The idea is similar to a regular treat ball but it's more challenging because the wobbler doesn't roll like a ball. In fact I'd recommend using a regular treat dispensing ball as an introduction to this type of toy. I've seen a number of dogs struggle with the Kong wobbler, mainly due to how it's been introduced. When you start off with this toy you must ensure it's got plenty of the dog's food inside (it works best with kibble). Otherwise the dog goes to the trouble of investigating the toy, pushing it around, but nothing comes out. Fortunately, the top part unscrews, so it's easy to fill. This feature also makes it easy to clean, unlike the traditional treat balls. The downside to this toy is that it's noisy as it bashes into furniture and walls. This could put many sensitive dogs off using it, so you might want to start off in the garden. If your dog is super good at the wobbler you could place a small ball inside to slow down the dispensing rate. But remember, enrichment is not about making life difficult, it's about making it interesting and enjoyable.

Chews: Chewing is undoubtedly a natural behaviour for dogs and helps to maintain healthy gums and teeth. There are hundreds of different products on the market, designed to fulfil the dog's love of chewing. Rawhide has probably been around the longest. It's certainly the only one I remember seeing as a child. Rawhide is basically a by-product of the leather industry consisting of the inner layer of animal skin. Due to the chemical processing methods used to produce the finished product many people have switched to more natural products. I don't like to tell people what to feed their dogs. Passions run high, there's not a diet on the market that everyone agrees on. But I don't think I know anyone in the dog training community who still advocates rawhide. That might ring some alarm bells. There are now lots of alternatives, so if you don't like the sound of rawhide, there's never been more to choose from. The problem with rawhide and other chew treats, for example, pigs' ears, is that they are designed to be a long lasting chew. Linda P. Case points out, in her excellent book, *Only Have Eyes For You,* that if the dog swallows a large chunk, it may not be fully digestible. Large chunks of undigested dog chew have the potential to cause an intestinal blockage. The long lasting chews are certainly fulfilling a natural behaviour, but we must always consider the risks. But before I scare you into depositing your chew stash into the nearest bin; I did a little research of my own. I asked 50 veterinarians and veterinary nurses how often they'd come across an intestinal blockage caused by long lasting chews. Most of them said it was quite rare and several had not had a single case in over 20 years of practice. In fact many volunteered the information that it was usually bones or non-food items that caused blockages. It isn't, by any stretch of the imagination, scientific research. It's more of a straw poll of vets and vet nurses I'm connected with via Facebook groups. It was rather reassuring, but not the end of the story. A few days after conducting my mini research project, the Center for

Disease Control & Prevention and the Food and Drug Administration in USA issued warnings that pigs ears shouldn't be fed to dogs as they were a likely cause of a salmonella outbreak in humans. If we consider the risks and still choose to feed these kinds of treats then excellent standards of food hygiene should be maintained at all times.

Bones: There's no doubt that dogs love a bone and that they can spend a long time chewing and gnawing at them. Firstly, cooked bones should never be fed to dogs, because they splinter. So if we're going to give bones, they should be raw bones. Even then, we should avoid ribs, pork bones and anything the dog could swallow whole. A big problem with raw bones is that people often forget about the importance of food hygiene around raw meat products. None of us would have a big chunk of raw meat hanging around and being transferred from surface to surface. We wouldn't leave raw meat out of the refrigerator for hours and we certainly wouldn't touch it without thoroughly cleaning our hands. Raw bones are also highly prized items to dogs so resource guarding may be a significant issue. I see lots of sterilized bones for sale with a hollow chamber running through the center. This is where the bone marrow once lived. I've seen these stuffed with food. The idea being that the dog has to work at getting it out. Unfortunately, I've also seen or heard of quite a few incidents of dogs getting their lower jaw stuck in the bone. This risk exists with any hollow centred bones. When I was young, our dogs always had large marrow bones and I don't ever remember there being any problems. However, taking all factors into account, I now choose not to give any bones to my dogs.

Nylabone: Nylabones may be a good alternative, but are far less appetising. They also don't come totally risk free and some people are concerned about giving non-edible (they definitely don't digest) products to dogs to chew on. It's possible that pieces could break off and be swallowed. They are designed to be slowly gnawed away at rather than large pieces breaking away. The only fragments I've seen coming off nylabones have been tiny specks, less than half the size of a grain of rice. If yours has bigger pieces coming away, I'd stop using it and purchase a new one. The nylabone should remain far too big to swallow. Don't let it become so worn that the dog could get the whole thing in his mouth or swallow it. In fact, keep it twice the size you think he could swallow.

Sleeping: Normally when I think about what's enriching, I'm thinking about things which activate and engage the brain. But in our quest to enrich their brain, we mustn't forget that dogs are amazingly good at sleeping. Most will sleep between 12 to 16 hours per day. It's not a solid sleep. It's more a series of short sleep and waking cycles, but they certainly spend much of their lives lazing around. This is probably one of the reasons they have successfully integrated into our lives so well. That doesn't mean you should get a dog with the expectations they will just sleep so can be left for long periods of time. Dogs love company, especially human company. We must also consider that dogs have been bred for many different functions and many breeds and individuals will certainly not be content to laze around for 16 hours. But how can we enrich this huge amount of time that dogs spend lying around? We can provide choices. Who choses the dogs sleeping spot? Well if they want their comfy bed, we probably do. We might have a bed in the kitchen or in the living room. But the dog doesn't necessarily sleep in the same room all the time.

Wouldn't it be nice to be able to wander off and choose their spot. They can do this, but usually it means losing their cosy bed. Why not have a bed in each room? Or at least two or three rooms. This gives real choice to the dog about where they choose to be. They can find the coolest or quietest spot whenever they want to.

Treasure Hunt: This is where we hide treats around the house and send the dog to find them. This game brings together the dog's superb scenting ability with the seeking system. The thrill of the chase is on. It's quite easy to teach a dog to go searching. I'd have a cue word just for this game. It's different from the search & rescue game because in this one he gets to eat what he finds.

Step 1: Let the dog see you put a treat down on the floor and allow him to get it. Maybe giving a cue word, such as 'search'. He doesn't really know what the word means yet, but as long as it comes just before he moves toward the treat, he'll soon learn that this word means, look for treats. It's easier if the dog already knows how to 'wait' so you can ask for a wait before placing the treat, but it's not essential. Repeat the exercise 10 times.

Step 2: Now start putting the treat where he can't actually see it, but he can see where you are putting it. For example, you could have a cushion on the floor and place a treat just to the far side of the cushion. Repeat 10 times and with varying objects, not just the cushion. Remember to use the cue word.

Step 3: Start to place the treat at times he can't see you doing it. Then give the cue word.

Step 4: Very slowly make the game more challenging by finding new places to hide the food. It should always be where he can access it. Never trick or tease him. If you want to hide treats in more than one place, start at the beginning again and let him see there is more than one location with treats. Maybe use two or three cushions on the floor and have treats behind each. I like to introduce another signal. When you know all the treats have been found, you could say 'All done' and give another piece of food. They soon learn that no more are to be found and they can relax.

Hol-ee Roller: This is a rubbery mesh ball. Actually it's quite a nice little toy by itself. My terrier loves shaking these about and they're not easily damaged. They can also be used as a food toy. Fleece strips can be tied all over the outside and then pushed inside. Drop some treats in there too so they're caught up in the fleece. Some dogs will just push the ball around like it's a treat ball. Others try to pull the fleece strips out to get to the treats. I often see large items pushed inside hol-ee rollers (because they stretch), for example a tennis ball. The dog often has no real hope of getting the toy out. Using it this way risks frustration rather than enrichment.

Kibble Bowling: Take a piece of kibble, one piece at a time and simply bowl it towards the dog as if it were a bowling ball. Or you can get on your knees and flick each piece toward the dog. It seems simple, and it is, but this game really sparks their brain. It's great for coordination and concentration. Inadvertently you are also teaching them to wait for your action. You get their full focus and bring the food to life.

Ten Green Buckets: Okay, they don't need to be green, or buckets, but it seemed like a catchy title. Take ten containers (I use small flexi-tubs) and stand them in a row. Stand at the end of the row and throw treats into the buckets. The dog's job is to find which bucket the treat landed in. To start this game just use two buckets and let the dog see you drop the treats in. You can then increase from there.

Ball Pit: You can use a child's ball pit or make your own with a paddling pool and quite a lot of ball pit balls. These balls are not made for dogs so great care should be taken that they don't chew and swallow them. You can have great fun hiding dog toys under the balls for the dog to find or you can sprinkle treats in the pit. The dog must then use his nose to sniff out where each piece of food is hiding. If you want to buy and store fewer balls, you can do the same thing with a large flexi tub.

Toilet Roll Tubes: Toilet roll tubes make great little packages for holding treats. Squash the end and fold the corners inwards; this prevents the tube from reopening. Place food inside the tube, then flatten the other end and fold the corners. If you flatten the end at a right angle to the first, the tube will be stronger, but it's not essential. You can use just one tube in the same way you might use a cereal box, just give it to the dog to open. However, if you collect the tubes for a while, you can play all sorts of games with them. With ten tubes you can lay them in a line, but only have food in one and the dog has to find which one. If you're feeling more ambitious, collect 50-100. Place all the tubes in a large box and let the dog find which one has the food inside. Most dogs will only damage the tubes containing the food; all the rest can be reused. Start off slow and easy with just one tube. If you don't fancy doing all that folding, don't bother, just lay the tubes out on the floor and place a treat in the centre. This will be a quicker exercise but he'll still be using his sense of smell to find which one has the treat. Absolutely ensure that your dog does not eat any of the cardboard tube.

Rucksack Walk: The rucksack walk consists of going for a short walk to a quiet open space where there are no pressures on the dog. In your rucksack (backpack) you take a scent item (maybe a herbal tea bag or some lavender), a special food item (maybe a little salmon), an interesting object (maybe a piece of plaited fleece) and a chew item. Find your quiet relaxing spot and let the dog have a sniff around on a long line. A long line is an extra long dog lead. Call them towards you a few times as you change position and drop a few treats by your feet. Sit down and slowly open the rucksack. With slow, deliberate movements, take out the tub containing the scent. You should only speak softly and act like the scent is something very special and interesting. Allow the dog to sniff the scent. It may help to have a lidded container with a few holes in the lid so they get plenty of scent without accessing the item. Slowly put the tub away and bring out the interesting item, in the same way. Let the dog explore and sniff it, but don't turn it into an exciting game; relax. Put the item away and bring out the special food. Feed this to them by hand if your dog is comfortable with that. Now bring out the chew. Just sit and relax while they eat the chew. That's it, time to go home, but keep it all relaxed.

The rucksack walk allows you both to relax outdoors and helps build connections and bonds between you both. It's being outside without any pressure to have to do this, that or the other. You might have gathered by now that in this book, I don't just give you the sunny side of life. Life's not all roses and no thorns. We must consider any risks. The risk here is the possibility of other dogs coming along as you are sitting relaxed with your dog happily chewing on the chew treat. With a food item and unknown dogs there is potential for trouble. Pick your quiet spot with this in mind. Ensure you can see if others are approaching rather than being surprised with a dog appearing a few metres away. You could even do the rucksack walk in a friend's garden where you can guarantee safety if you're unable to find a space you are happy with. The rucksack walk was devised by, dog trainer, Steve Mann. Steve writes about this, and much more, in his book, *Easy Peasy Puppy Squeezy*.

Treat Trail: This is extremely simple to do. Set up a trail of food treats around the house or garden for the dog to follow. I place them at intervals of about 15 centimetres. Use a third of the dog's daily food allowance and the trail can get really long. If you're not that keen in setting them all up, just do about 20 kibble pieces. If you feed raw or wet food, you might need to consider dehydrated treats, but remember to reduce the daily food allowance if you are adding extras. Enrichment doesn't need to be overly complex. I love the simple activities and we're more likely to keep them up.

Toy Box Delight: If your dog has a toy box full of different toys, you can put it to extra use and drop a handful of treats in there. Remember to start off easy. Maybe with just a few toys in the box.

Garden Centre: It can be difficult to find places where dogs are permitted, other than the local park or field. But garden centres are often happy to allow dogs. All those new plant smells will give plenty of sniffing opportunities. Keep visits short to start with so that the dog is not overwhelmed. You could start with 5 minutes and build it up to 20 minutes over a few days. If dogs only ever see the local field, it can be stressful for them when you need to go to other places.

Varying their experience with safe environments will not only enrich their lives but also equip them with the ability to better cope in new environments.

Training: Is training enrichment? I get asked this a lot. Generally I avoid promoting training as enrichment because there are so many aspects of training which wouldn't be enriching. For example, choke chains (also known as check chains) could never be classed as enrichment. Whether it's the tightening of the chain or merely the chink it makes, the objective is to stop the dog doing something based on him not liking the chinking or tightening of the chain. It's not only aversive tools that prevent training being enriching. It could be a nice friendly training class. If your dog is stressed by being in the class then it's not enrichment. Enrichment must be enjoyable; it must be something the dog wants. I'm not suggesting that you never go to a training class. Good instructors will be looking out for stress and doing all they can to alleviate it and turn the class into a positive experience for you and your dog. But in my many years on this earth I've frequented a lot of classes and seen lots of training videos. I've seen dogs shouted at, sprayed in the face with water, forced into a down position, forced to stay next to unfamiliar dogs. I've even seen a video of a training class where fireworks were let off right next to the dogs, who were forced not to run away. Never mind enrichment, that's outright animal abuse. None of these things are enrichment. If we want training to be enriching then we need to make it enriching. Just like with any of the other enrichment activities, we must start off really easy and we must make it enjoyable for the dog. The search and rescue exercise described earlier is a perfect example of training which is also enrichment. Each stage is positive and rewarding for the dog. The same can be said for the recall guide and my approach to resource guarding. There's no pressure and the dog doesn't realise he's even training. This isn't a training manual and I'll resist turning it into one but almost anything you could ever want to teach a companion dog can be done using these positive and enriching methods. I know there may be a lot of readers thinking, 'not with my dog'. But I've not come across a dog training situation yet that couldn't be improved by using positive reinforcement and kindness. Dog training has a long history of less kind training methods but I hope one day that all training will be enriching for the dog and not merely to serve a human need.

Meeting People: Lots of people like to say hello to dogs, but recently in the dog training community there's been a growing resentment to people who come over to pat the dog. I've read countless angry posts (and even some videos) about it. They normally begin with something like,

"NO, IT'S NOT OKAY TO TOUCH MY DOG!"

The reason behind this attitude is that many dogs may have fear issues. Even without fear issues, most dogs don't want a stranger's hands all over their head. Approaching face on is also a little intimidating or challenging to dogs. When it comes to dogs, humans are slow learners. How has it taken 20,000 (ish) years of domestication for us to realise that dogs don't actually like being patted on the head, and certainly not by a stranger. But here's the thing; people are going to do it anyway. They're going to come over to pat your dog. Hopefully most will ask first. If you really don't want them to, that's fine, it's your job to look after the dog and keep him safe. But are we missing the opportunity for the dog to become accustomed to people sometimes coming over to say hi? Are we missing the opportunity to help inform people of dogs' preferences? We could try something like this;

Stranger: Hi, can I stroke your dog?

You: Just stand still and let him sniff you, this helps dogs to feel safe. They can feel afraid if people suddenly touch them.

Stranger: Oh, really? Okay

You: Now just gently pat his shoulder; dogs really don't like hands coming towards their face.

You: You've made his day, thank you.

This isn't suitable for all dogs. But if they are completely human friendly and not stressed or anxious it can be a rather nice enrichment opportunity. Safety must absolutely be your first priority. If there is any risk of people being injured by touching or getting too close you need to be thinking about management. Think about using a muzzle (this can also be trained positively so the dog associates it with good things) and don't get into a situation where a problem could occur. If you need to say no to people wanting to say hi, you need to be assertive, but without being rude.

Stranger: Hi, Can I stroke your dog?

You: Sorry, no, he gets afraid

Stranger: It's okay I'm good with dogs

You: You're helping by not touching him. Thank you.

Just Me and my Dog: Enrichment isn't about keeping dogs occupied for eight hours per day. On the contrary, many activities take just a few minutes. Little and often is a very good strategy for providing enrichment without frustration creeping in. Dogs don't need to be on the go all day, they just love being with us. Spend plenty of time just relaxing with them. Give light gentle strokes as you sit watching TV or reading a book. In the dog training community, I'm what they might call a foodie. I use the dog's food for most of their training. I also use food for lots of enrichment. For safety reasons, don't hold your breath waiting for me to apologise for being a foodie. Animals need food, that's what makes food a primary reinforcer. But they need other things too, like safety and companionship. We don't want life to be all about food. Spend plenty of time just relaxing and giving gentle touches and strokes. If all your interactions involve food you may get into a situation where you can't even pet your canine companion without them looking for food rather than enjoying the interaction.

Yes, But ....

There's always a 'yes, but'. We fill our lives with 'yes, but'. So this section of the book is dedicated to answering some of the most frequent yes, buts.

My dog's just too smart

I've often heard people complain that their dog has completed every challenge, so there's nothing left for them to do. They're just too smart for enrichment!

Enrichment isn't a one-time challenge. It's not really a challenge at all; it's an interesting and enjoyable activity. If the activity is interesting and enjoyable, why wouldn't the dog gain benefit from doing it again and again. If the dog has been successful in the past, he will be very happy to see the toy again. It's good to introduce new activities, but the completed ones are far from finished with. I use Kongs, Pickpocket Foragers and K9 Connectables almost daily. My dogs have completed them thousands of times. Their brains still spark into life when they see them and they still get immense pleasure from interacting with them.

My dog has no interest in food toys

If your dog has a normal appetite when eating from a bowl, but will not put any effort into getting food from food toys, there are a few possible reasons. They're fearful, don't know what to do, or lack motivation. It could also be a combination of the three.

Fearful: How a dog behaves is very much based on their past experiences. If they've been harshly punished for investigating new items, this may affect their willingness to investigate in the future. It doesn't take much stretching of the imagination to see how this might happen, even in a loving environment. Shouting, panicking, grabbing the dog and pulling something out of their mouth or yelling at them for chewing the TV remote. These things can cause dogs to shut down in fear of being punished. Dogs much prefer calm humans. But humans are humans. We get annoyed and grumpy and panicky and upset. We need to be aware of this and do all we can not to take our frustrations out on the dog, who after all, is always just being a dog. We need to teach the dog they're safe to explore enrichment items. We need to cease anything which causes physical or emotional discomfort and allow the dog to feel completely safe with us.

Don't know what to do: There's food in your cupboards and fridge right now isn't there? We know without a shadow of a doubt that dogs can smell minute aromas. They know the food is in your cupboards, yet they almost never bother trying to get to it. They might learn this if you left the cupboard open with some easy pickings inside. But generally they don't bother with it. They know it's not accessible to them. So it's not that surprising that they may also not bother with a food toy if it seems that the food is inaccessible to them. We need to simplify. Make the food ridiculously easy to access to start with and build up the level of required effort later. Remember to take baby steps. If we are failing then we've set the bar too high.

Motivation: This word is used frequently in the dog world, but what does it really mean and how do we go about increasing motivation? Motivation is the willingness to commence and maintain behaviour toward (or away from) stimuli in order to meet physical and/or psychological needs or desires. Simply put, there needs to be something the dog wants.

The dog may usually be fed from a bowl. They may actually be overfed if nobody's weighing the food. Do they really need or want a few extra pieces of kibble in a dog toy. This is hugely dependent on the individual dog. Some, like my Lab, Mr B., would absolutely want a few extra pieces of kibble. My West Highland Terrier, Miss Daisy, wouldn't be too fussed. There are a few things we can do to increase motivation. We could use a food that has a higher motivational value. A few slices of sausage would do the job for most dogs. However, we must be careful not to add too many calories. It's fine to add a few treats to increase motivation and interest but we certainly don't need to be filling food toys with extra special treats.

Feed a good quality food as the dog's main diet and use this food for most of their enrichment. Food enrichment is never about extra food, it's about providing their food in more interesting ways. If we ensure we're not overfeeding and we stop feeding from a bowl, the dog should naturally gain motivation to interact with food enrichment toys. This is not a case of forcing dogs to work for food. We're only attempting to make feeding more interesting to them, as it should be. It doesn't need to be difficult. You could simply start with scatter feeding or flicking food across the floor. If you have weighed the food in the morning you'll be able to keep track of how much is being eaten. Anything left over could be given in the evening. We must ensure that the dog gets their daily food allowance regardless of enrichment activities. It must also be considered that not all enrichment will suit all dogs. For example, many of the more sensitive dogs may not enjoy noisy enrichment toys. Often we may need to try several different activities to learn what our dogs really love doing. Motivation isn't all about food though. Miss Daisy has never been highly motivated by food unless it is something super high value. Squeak a squeaky toy however and she is there at lightning speed. Sometimes it's about finding what rocks their world.

Will enrichment teach them to be destructive?

People are often concerned that encouraging dogs to rip up items such as cardboard boxes will teach them to also destroy other things in the home. It seems a logical connection to make; however, dogs are experts at noticing every move we make. They're expert at knowing what pays and what doesn't. And they're expert at noticing context. If you feed your dog a few leftovers from dinner plates, they soon learn to eagerly follow you to the kitchen. They didn't need formal training for this; they just know that it sometimes pays to follow you with the dinner plate when you've just eaten. Walk around the house with clean plate and they're not very interested. Leave the washed plates on the draining board and the dog pays no attention whatsoever. They understand the context of when that dinner plate might be significant to them.

In many years of giving my dogs cardboard boxes to destroy, never have they attempted to access a box not meant for them. This of course doesn't mean that a dog will not destroy things which you wanted to keep. It means only that using boxes in enrichment is not teaching them to destroy all boxes, just as letting them walk into your house isn't teaching them to walk into all houses. When the food item has gone, I always tidy the box away. Once the food or toy has been found, I remove the box. The game is to access the items in the box, not simply the destruction of the box. This allows a clear focus and objective rather than the general destruction of boxes for no clear purpose. It's prudent to keep valuables (or boxes you want to keep) out of the dog's reach. Remember to consider the risks: are there any toxins on the box? will the dog eat bits of box? is the glue safe? You should also supervise at all times.

My dog doesn't like going for walks

There are many reasons that a dog may not enjoy the outside world. They may have undiagnosed pain or discomfort. They may be fearful and anxious due to previous events in their lives. They may not be comfortable with the feel of the collar being pulled against the neck. Perhaps the human gets anxious and this makes the dog anxious. Perhaps they were not introduced to the outside world appropriately as a puppy. I could write a book on the number of reasons, but the fact is, the dog isn't comfortable with going for a walk, at least not in the usual context. If they are not comfortable with it, it certainly isn't enrichment. There are still hundreds of enriching activities you can do at home. The idea that dogs need a one hour walk each day is not correct. It's never going to be appropriate for all dogs. For millions of dogs it's fantastic to get outside and take in all these scents and sounds, but for some, it could be an act of cruelty. If you have a dog who's afraid of the outside world you could consider working with a properly qualified behaviourist. An appropriate approach would include offering the dog choices. It might include just allowing the dog to step outside and return. Even this may not be the first step, because the dog probably associates the lead and harness with going outside and this would need to be worked on first. Not going for regular walks isn't a reason to forget about enrichment, it's a reason to do more.

My dogs will fight over toys or food

It's not unusual for dogs to get physically competitive around highly prized items. The answer is to allow dogs to feel safe and secure that their item is not going to be taken. This is done by giving each dog a secure space away from the other dogs. My dogs have never had a fight with each other or any other dog. But when I do food enrichment I still separate them. We don't want competition creeping in. We don't want them speeding up to eat as much as they can before the other dogs gets it. We want them to relax and enjoy their enrichment. It's not enrichment if you're worried about your prize being taken. In addition, separate enrichment makes it far easier to keep track of how much each dog has eaten of their daily allowance.

How much enrichment is too much?

Enrichment activities should create interest and be enjoyable. But behaviour doesn't occur in a vacuum. Everything is dependent on everything else. Imagine your dog's favourite activity is chasing pieces of his favourite food being flicked across the kitchen floor. The laws of physics dictate that the dog can't eat continuously. At some point they reach satiation. They've eaten all the food they need or want. Now motivation will rapidly decline. It's not just the food. Any physical or mental activity, if not ceased while it is still pleasurable, will eventually reach satiation. There's a cliché you could hardly have missed; a tired dog is a happy dog. But this cliché is utter nonsense. A tired dog is a tired dog. That is all. We can't assume all tired dogs are happy. I imagine a dog used in the barbaric act of dog fighting gets pretty tired but we wouldn't call them happy. Enrichment isn't to tire dogs out. It's to give them an interesting and enjoyable life. A sniffing walk can take me an hour. A well stuffed classic Kong could take about 10 - 15 minutes (longer if frozen). But most activities last no longer than 10 minutes and many can be a couple of minutes. The longer an activity lasts, especially where the objective is to access food, the greater the risk of it becoming frustrating for the dog. Keep activities short. Our objective isn't to get anywhere near satiation, it's just to create interest and enjoyment. There are of course, some working breeds (and individuals of other breeds) that have a much higher need for physical and mental stimulation. These dogs usually do best with guardians who participate in dog sports. They crave a busier life and far more stimulation than the average companion dog. For example, Belgian Malinois and Border Collies are not easily fulfilled in our modern and often sedentary lives.

My dog's too lazy

What does lazy mean? Lazy means unwilling to work or make an effort. Why would a dog be unwilling to work or make an effort? This brings us back to a lack of motivation. If a dog is getting enough (or too much) food elsewhere, without effort then there may be reduced motivation. But what if we're not talking about food toys? What if we're talking about a flirt pole or fetch? If your dog isn't interested, it may be that these things are just not his kind of thing. Some of the very stocky breeds, for example, Bulldog and Bullmastiff, expend much more energy chasing things. This will undoubtedly affect motivation. They do often run around and play but we must be realistic in our expectations and differentiate activities to suit them. They can't behave like Border Collies, no matter how highly valued the prize.

Lazy could also be a misinterpretation. Perhaps the dog is actually anxious, fearful or confused. If you think your dog is not behaving normally for their breed type or if they've suddenly become less motivated to move around, you should always get a veterinarian to check them over. People frequently skip this step. They don't want to pay out in case it's nothing serious. But the dog can't tell us when something's wrong so we need to be proactive; we need to be looking for it. My right shoulder gave me pain for over a year. There were many things I couldn't do. I couldn't lift my right arm very high, not even enough to wash my armpit. I couldn't even lift the arm across my body to wash under the other armpit. To everyone else, I looked fine. When the arm was down and relaxed there was no pain. As long as my arm was pointing down, I could even carry heavy shopping. But using the arm in a raised position was excruciating. Scans revealed arthritis in the shoulder and it was successfully treated with physio and a steroid injection. But dogs get joint and muscle problems too. How would they tell us? How long would they suffer before we noticed? Would we ever notice? Would we just call them lazy? Get to know your dog. Really take notice of how they move. Give very slow gentle and relaxed strokes, noticing any areas where they are not so keen on being touched. I don't much like the word lazy. It seems like an insult. It is often said lovingly, but even then, it's a great big unhelpful label which

82

screams '*I don't have to bother working out what's going on, he's just lazy*'. If we do that, perhaps it is us who are lazy.

I need things that will last all day

Surprisingly often I'm asked, 'what enrichment item will last all day?' The question usually relates to dogs which are left all day while the human goes to work. It very often also relates to separation distress or anxiety of some degree. I could give the somewhat flippant answer of, 'you'. If the dog is alone all day and suffering separation anxiety, it's not because he wants an eight hour snuffle mat; it's because he wants you. That's not really a very helpful answer because that's exactly what many people can't provide. There's no quick fix that I know of. It's extremely difficult for dogs and humans. But these issues need professional assessment and guidance. Separation distress isn't fixable by merely providing a few enrichment toys.

It may be that the dog doesn't have any major distress. It may be that you just want them to have something to do while you're out. But do we really want dogs to be active when we're out? My advice is usually to teach dogs to settle while they're left alone. The more activity, the more there's risk of injury. Because of this risk, the vast majority of enrichment toys are not intended to be used without human supervision. Our best option is more likely one of ensuring the dog has had some physical and mental stimulation before being left.

He destroys every toy I give him

Dogs destroy toys because that's often where the stimulation is. They think that's the whole point of the game. If you are using a food toy, make the game really easy to start with so that the dog's focus is on the food. You could spread wet food over the outer surface and increase the level of difficulty from there. The dog should learn that the stimulation is in getting the food, not destroying the toy. When the food is finished, take the dog's mind off the toy with some other games, maybe a treasure hunt, or scatter feeding. You can remove the toy whilst he is doing other things. He shouldn't even notice you take the toy. I don't take things from dogs without first occupying them with something else. The food toys are not usually designed to be left laying around for the dog to chew at will.

But what about the non-food toys? The shops that sell these toys often display notices stating, these toys are not indestructible. This is because they often have returns from unhappy customers who just paid good money for a toy that lasted no more than a day. If you have a dog who instantly destroys his toys, you are not alone. That's why the shop has the sign. It would cost them too much money to keep exchanging items or refunding. Chewing is an innate behaviour in dogs, it's a genetic predisposition. Your dog's not defective or naughty, he's just being a dog. If dogs were made to chew, then yours is doing a great job.

There are toys that are particularly good at standing up to tough chewers, for example, Nylabone, Kong Extreme, GoughNuts or West Paw (these are tough but nothing is truly indestructible). There are things we can do to alter how

84

the dog interacts with the toy. Don't just give the toy to the dog and walk away. Watch how he interacts with it. If he thinks the fun is in chewing it up then that's what he's going to do. Maybe stick around and make the toy fun in other ways, like chasing it around, playing fetch or tug. If you have difficulty getting the toy back from the dog, have two identical toys. Play with your dog using one toy. When you want him to leave it, make the other toy the interesting one by playing with that one and paying no attention to the dog's original toy. They often want what somebody else has and will leave their toy to play with the interesting one (it's your job to make it the interesting one). You can keep swapping and making them fun. When you're finished, you could end with some scatter feeding and remove the toys without them noticing. If you want something super durable they can chew on, I'd recommend the GoughNuts range.

How do I know if my dog is enjoying it or getting frustrated?

We often assume something is enrichment, but it's only enrichment if the dog finds it enriching. How do we know whether the dog is enjoying the process or finding it frustrating? There's a fine line between enjoyment and frustration. What was enjoyable one minute can soon become frustrating in another minute. Imagine the dog is playing with a treat dispensing ball. Each time they roll the ball treats fall out. Dogs quickly learn when there are no treats left because the treats are no longer rattling around. But if the treats are still inside but the hole has become blocked, the dog will not be successful. The behaviour that's always worked is no longer working. The dog will try harder, perhaps hitting the ball with more force and upping the pace. Nothing pays off. This is frustration. In human terms, imagine you enter your workplace through the same unlocked door every day. One day, you reach for the handle, push it down, and nothing. The door's locked! Nobody ever just walks away. We try it again. We try harder. We try faster. Nothing works. We don't understand, we're confused and we're frustrated. If a toy is supposed to deliver food, then that's what it ought to do. The dog should be winning. We're not trying to outsmart him; we're making him a winner. And who doesn't enjoy winning?

Contrary to popular belief, dogs are not great at solving puzzles. There are a number of complex puzzles on the market but they usually require us to teach the dog each step. I've seen examples where the dog has to pull out a little drawer to access the food inside. The process of introducing such a toy would be to present it with the drawers open. Then three-quarters open, then half open, quarter open then almost closed, then closed. If we presented it with the drawer closed the dog would possibly work it out, but it would be through trial and error of bashing the toy about until something paid off. They wouldn't instantly know what it was that they did so this would take a number of attempts before learning took place. Now imagine the toy has a locking mechanism for each drawer. A slider must be moved before the dog can open each drawer. This is beyond the capabilities of most, if not all, dogs. We could quite easily teach them the process, but left to their own devices it would take a lot of good luck and even more frustration. There's nothing wrong with these puzzles, they can add interest and promote fine motor skills, but it is a case of teaching the process (or behaviour chain) rather than them solving a puzzle. If the dog's bashing it about or repeatedly pawing at it and not getting any success, then this is frustration. Set them up to be successful, and frustration will not get a foot in the door.

We can also judge what our dogs enjoy by giving them choices. Do they really like the way you play with them, or do they just tolerate it? Try playing with them for just five or ten seconds, then stop. Do they move away when given the opportunity, or do they initiate further contact? The clues are there. Dogs are always telling us, but if we don't give them choices, they can't choose.

My dog is on crate rest, what can we do?

There are many reasons a dog might be on crate rest. Crate rest is often prescribed following surgery or injury. It's therefore vital that you discuss with the veterinarian prescribing crate rest, what the dog may or may not do. Stimulating a dog whilst on crate rest can be challenging. Remember that some movements may be uncomfortable and the dog is probably not his usual self. Medications can also influence how dogs learn and respond so be sure to discuss medication side effects with your veterinarian. Low impact activities which may be suitable include snuffle mats, Kongs, and licki mats. Even though I don't usually find licki mats to be highly enriching, on crate rest, they may be a welcome distraction. Play simple games which don't require too much effort. One such game is putting treats in a pudding baking tray and then placing balls on top. It's not too challenging for dogs to move the balls and find the treats. Train simple behaviours, such as hand touch. Hold the flat of your hand to the side of the dogs face. Your palm should be facing the dog's face, but not straight on. Most dogs will give a little sniff of the hand. As they do, say 'yes', and give a treat. Before long you will be able to move your hand around into different positions and get the dog to touch the palm with his nose. You can also introduce a cue word such as 'touch', as you hold out you hand, but don't add the cue word until he is doing it every time without the word. If the dog doesn't naturally sniff your hand at the start of training, try rubbing something nice on there, such as cheese. If the dog can't go outside you could bring interesting things for him to sniff. You can also use this time for bonding with your dog. If he is happy for you to do so, sit next to him, talk to him, gently stroke him. Let him know you are in this together. During crate rest, dogs should be kept calm. Enrichment comes second place. First place must be following your veterinarian's advice.

My dog is old

Life is the process of getting old. There's no age at which life suddenly becomes unenjoyable. Lots of older people begin hobbies, start small businesses and go back to college after retirement age. Why should dogs be any different? It's merely about finding suitable activities. A twelve year old dog isn't going to take up flyball, but they can certainly enjoy their retirement years, wandering around sniffing. You can take shorter walks and just take in the environment. While they are still enjoying activities, keep doing them. If they are slowing down or finding things difficult, we just simplify things. For example we might place food in a Kong very lightly so it easily falls out. Caring for an older dog shouldn't feel like a burden. It should be our privilege. We have the ability to alter things so they can continue to enjoy life. To have the power to improve another being's life it truly a great privilege. But don't just assume they can't do things. My twelve year old, Miss Daisy, is still running around enjoying life like she's a puppy.

My dog is just a puppy

There's no reason a puppy shouldn't enjoy enrichment activities. However, with puppies, it is more than the enrichment factor.

If we want to raise dogs who are comfortable and confident, then, ideally, they need early, fear free, introduction to the environments they may face during their lifetime. This can be problematic because the most influential learning stage (traditionally known as the secondary socialisation period) of a puppies life is approximately 4 - 12 weeks of age. Because of vaccination guidance, our puppies are usually kept safely away from the outside world at this age. This is hugely unfortunate. I never tell people to go against veterinary advice. Sometimes vets get a bad rap. Time and time again, I've seen social media posts criticising veterinarians. Things like, they know nothing about animal behaviour or they know nothing about diet. Another common misconception is that they don't know about psychoactive medications. Certainly, vets in general practice don't specialise in these areas. But veterinarians are at the front line. They are the ones dealing with the consequences of our actions. They are the ones who must euthanise companion animals because of our neglect. I have the utmost respect for the veterinary profession. But our vaccination schedules and the dog's need to learn about the outside world, clash terribly. That's not to say we can't raise great dogs whilst following the guidelines. We're not all walking around with a fearful or unsociable dog. As always, dogs vary tremendously and some will be more greatly affected than others. I do all I can to introduce puppies to the outside world, even if it means carrying them. Don't go against veterinarian advice, consult with them. Discuss what might be acceptable ways for your pup to experience the outside world before the secondary socialisation period is over.

The socialisation period aside, we can provide enrichment at home. But again, it's prudent to be considering things from the perspective of learning. Introduce different materials, sounds and scents. I don't really think about an enrichment need with pups. I think about a learning need. Forget about puzzles, they don't need puzzles; they need to learn about the human world they've been brought into. Forget about tiring them out, they don't need tiring out. Growing and playing and learning are quite tiring enough. In case you didn't read the entire book, I'll say it again, puppies are not miniature dogs, they're babies. Be gentle, be calm and be a place of safety. There are lots of toys they can have, and they generally love anything that moves. The flirt poles can be fantastic because they get something to chase and the human can let their hands recover from those pin sharp teeth and nails. But we must resist doing too much and definitely no jumping. The growth plates of the long bones may not close until around eighteen months of age. These immature bones may not be able to withstand the high impact or repetitive forces of some activities such as agility, catching discs or over enthusiastic chasing of the flirt pole.

It's too expensive to buy the enrichment toys

It's true, some of them are expensive. But we don't need a single manufactured enrichment toy to enrich our dogs. They're nice to have. It's nice to go to the enrichment cupboard and decide what we're going to use. But it's far from essential. Here's the secret, dogs don't care about how much things cost. Take them to a forest and they will be in their absolute element. Chuck some kibble in an empty cereal box. Wrap some food in a towel, spend five minutes playing with them or giving belly rubs. Roll their food across the floor to them, go on a sniffari. The best enrichment doesn't come in an expensive box, it comes from an interactive, caring and compassionate relationship.

My dog will get fat

Never, no, absolutely not. I've been providing my dogs' food via enrichment for 20 years and I've never had an overweight dog. Weigh out their food allowance in the morning. Use this food for enrichment feeding. Enrichment feeding is never about providing extra calories. It's about feeding their main diet in more interesting ways.

Does mental stimulation replace physical activity?

It's become a common belief that mental stimulation is better for dogs than physical activity. For example, I recently read a snuffle mat manufacturer's claim that ten minutes of sniffing equals one hour of running. I'm not sure how they reached this conclusion but we must be sure to apply a good dose of scepticism to any such claims. Physical exercise is vitally important for maintaining physical fitness. I'm well known for my promotion of mental stimulation, but nobody ever got physically fitter by doing crossword puzzles or sitting at a desk. No amount of mental stimulation can replace the need for physical activity. And no amount of physical activity can replace the need for mental stimulation.

I just don't have the time

Many people will read this and think, how can you not have time for your dog? But in reality and despite ever more inventions designed to save us time, we are often time poor.

91

I'm sure we'd love to play with dogs all day but that's not the reality of life for most people. We have busy lives, that's a fact. But that's not a get out of jail free card. It doesn't free us of our responsibilities. A busy life doesn't need to prevent us improving the dog's life. There are some very simple things we can incorporate into our daily lives.

- Weigh their food at the weekend and keep it in containers for each day

- Take them for 5 minute sniffs outside. Longer might be better but several 5 minute sniffs make a much better life than none

- Keep the food container close at hand, every so often shout, 'cowabunga' (but not so loud the you startle the dog or make the neighbours think you're reliving the 80's) and throw some treats on the floor

- Each and every time you make a cup of tea, use the time while the kettle boils to do things with your dogs

- Chuck some treats in an empty cereal box and let the dog get them out

- Place food in different areas of the living room for a quick treasure hunt

- Play catch by chucking treats to the dog

- Grab a soft tug toy and have a one minute gentle play

- Don't just walk past the dog, instead, stop and give them ten seconds of fuss

- Have a few special treats in the fridge. This could be some of your leftovers from dinner. When the dog does a behaviour you love, say 'yes' and run them to the fridge for a special treat. We're talking no more than a teaspoon full

- Give them a small carrot when you get home from work

- Sit with them to watch TV and give a gentle massage

- Stuff a Kong, leave it in the fridge and let them have it while you eat dinner

- Wrap treats in a tea-towel and give it to the dog

- Place treats in a cardboard tube and fold the ends over

- Stand in another room and squeak a squeaky toy until the dog comes to find you. Chuck the toy for them

- Put a treat under a cushion for them to find. Let them see you place it, then encourage them to find it

- Have a gentle wrestle with them

- It doesn't have to be complex. What the dog needs most is you. Build small interactions into your daily routine. We can't all do everything. But we can all do something

The Final Word

If you could choose your own guardian angel, what kind of angel would you choose? Would you choose a selfish or inconsiderate one who does whatever they please without ever considering your wants or needs?

Or

Would you choose a kind, considerate guardian angel who looks out for you, keeps you safe, and ensures you get your share of the good times?

The question is ridiculous. Not because guardian angels are mythical (allegedly), but because the answer is obvious. We would all choose the kind and considerate angel.

What kind of guardian angel would you choose for your dog? This time you really do get to choose because your dog's guardian angel is you.

I sincerely hope you found this book interesting and useful.

Please stop by at **facebook.com/canineenrichmentbook** and let me know how it's helped you.

You may also like to visit the Canine Enrichment group for more enrichment ideas.
facebook.com/groups/canineenrichment/

Please note that I am not affiliated with any other groups or pages which have similar names.

May you and your dog enrich each other's lives. Thank you for reading.

Shay Kelly

About the author

Shay Kelly is a canine behaviour advisor with a passion for improving the dog-human relationship through stimulating enrichment activities.

Undeterred by an ineffective early education, Shay's quest for knowledge saw him go on to graduate at the age of 51 from Bishop Burton College in collaboration with the University of Hull. There he achieved a First Class result in BSc Canine Behaviour Management.

Shay was never going to be a typical university student. Whilst respectfully challenging lecturers at every opportunity, his studies saw him receive the Ian McParland award for the greatest personal achievement and a 100% grade in advanced dog training.

His behavioural qualifications, Buddhist values, and utter refusal to take anything at face value combine to deliver science-based behavioural advice which is, above all else, kind and ethical.

If They Could Only Speak

They say that dogs are loyal
I don't always agree
They have no other option
They can't just leave or run free
~

We bring them into our lives
They don't have a choice
The dog does not complain
Because they do not have a voice
~

They can't pack a bag
Or slip away by night
They must stay whatever
And simply face their plight
~

Their life is based on chance
A roll of the dice
Live with someone horrid
Or live with someone nice
~

Dogs depend on us
And what we choose to give
How we meet their needs
Decides how happily they live
~

Don't we owe it to them
To do the best we can
And give them all they need
To better live with man
~

We can give so much more
Than water, warmth and food
There are many activities
We could and should include
~

Give the dog an interest
Something they enjoy
Like playing with a doggy friend
Or a box they can destroy
~

Take them to the river
To the fields and through the mud
Let them be a dog
And do the things dogs should
~

Let them play and run
And sniff and then to seek
Give them all the things they'd ask for
If they could only speak
~

~ Shay Kelly ~

Printed in Great Britain
by Amazon